RICHARD PORSON

RICHARD PORSON AET. 37

from the portrait by Hoppner in the Old Schools

RICHARD PORSON

A BIOGRAPHICAL ESSAY

BY

M. L. CLARKE

FELLOW OF KING'S COLLEGE

CAMBRIDGE

AT THE UNIVERSITY PRESS
1937

CONTENTS

PLATES

PREFACE

NONE of those who knew Porson personally wrote about him at length, and the office of biographer was left to the unhappy John Selby Watson, whose *Life of Porson* appeared in 1861. It is an undistinguished compilation, and its inadequacy has led me to hope that a new book on the subject will not be considered otiose. But no account of Porson is likely to be wholly satisfactory, because of the poor quality of the original sources. Porson, it has been said, had his Mrs Piozzi, but not his Boswell. But the *Porsoniana* of Maltby and Barker cannot compare in quality even with the *Anecdotes of Johnson*. Too much of the material for Porson's life consists of mere scraps of anecdote and reminiscence.

There is seldom any means of testing the accuracy of anecdotes. One must admit their unreliability, and comfort oneself with the reflection that though they may not be strictly accurate, they are unlikely to be far removed from the truth. If I have not always thought it worth while to preface a story with 'It is said that...', or some such phrase, I hope I shall not be considered unduly credulous.

As John Selby Watson remarked in his preface, 'the life of such a scholar could hardly be written without exhibiting in its pages some portions of Latin and Greek'. There is then no need for apology on this point; perhaps I should rather apologise for not discussing more fully questions of scholarship. But besides requiring more learning than I possess, such a discussion could not easily be fitted into a book of this scale. Perhaps some day the subject of Porson's scholarship will be treated for the benefit of scholars by some one better qualified for the task than I am; meanwhile I may repeat Watson's modest, though I fear vain hope, that 'the book is of such a nature on the whole as to be no unacceptable offering to the literary world'.

My thanks are due to the Council of Trinity College for permission to print unpublished letters of Porson belonging to the college, and to use and quote from other manuscript material; also for permission to reproduce specimens of Porson's handwriting from his manuscripts. I am grateful also to Mr John Sparrow, who has allowed me to print the letters whose originals he possesses, and to others who have given information and assistance. In particular I am indebted to Professor D. S. Robertson, who has suggested some improvements, and to the Rev. H. W. Moule, who has read the proofs.

M. L. C.

1937

I

EAST RUSTON is a scattered and poor village in Norfolk, some five miles to the south-east of North Walsham, in a flat district not far from the sea. Here Richard Porson was born on Christmas Day, 1759. His parents were poor, but not illiterate. His father, Huggin Porson, a worsted-weaver by trade, was son of the parish clerk, and on his father's death, as often happened, succeeded to the clerkship. A few years before this he had married Ann Palmer, the daughter of a shoemaker of Catfield,[1] a village about five miles to the south-east. From her, so it was believed, rather than from his father, Porson derived his ability. She is described as clever and lively, and had been able to gratify her taste for reading when in service at a gentleman's house.

Their children numbered seven,[2] of whom four reached maturity. Of these the second was Richard, named, in Greek fashion, after his grandfather. The other three surviving children had intelligence above the average and were able to attain to respectable positions in the world. Henry, born next after Richard, became an exciseman and farmer; Thomas, who was considered

[1] So the parish register. Of Bacton, according to the printed accounts of Porson.
[2] Elizabeth b. 1756, d. 1842, John b. 1757, d. 1761, Richard b. 1759, d. 1808, Henry b. 1761, d. 1795, John b. 1764, ? died young, Huggin b. 1766, died in infancy, Thomas b. 1770, d. 1792. Mrs Porson died in 1784 and her husband in 1806. Their gravestone may be seen on the south of East Ruston church, near the east end of the nave.

by some equal in ability to Richard, though he had less education, became a schoolmaster first at Wymondham then at Fakenham, but died at the age of twenty-two. The only daughter, Elizabeth, the eldest of the family, started life in service, but afterwards married her employer, a brewer called Siday Hawes, and lived at Coltishall, a village between Norwich and North Walsham. A memorial inscription records that 'She had by nature a strong and capacious mind, which she found time to cultivate amidst the hardships of her early life, and the various employments of her later years; whilst her pity and benevolence made her take delight in relieving the sufferings of the poor, for she had both seen and felt what those sufferings were. And thus to the day of her Death, she shared her own prosperity with the class from which she sprang.'

For a short time Richard Porson attended the village school at Bacton, about four miles to the north, which was kept by one John Woodrow, but he was a weakly boy, and unable to stand the company of the rough village lads, and so was removed after a month or two. In his father's cottage there were one or two mathematical books,[1] and from these he taught himself some arithmetic, so that when he next went to school he could already extract a cube root. At the age of nine he began to attend the Free School at the neighbouring village of Happisburgh. His father evidently had no thought of his becoming a scholar. 'I have brought my son Richard to you', he said to Mr Summers, the

[1] Also the Bible, Jewel's *Apology*, Greenwood's *English Grammar*, an odd volume of Chambers's *Encyclopaedia* picked up from a wrecked coaster, and eight or ten volumes of *The Universal Magazine*.

schoolmaster, 'and just want him to make (i.e. write) his name, and then I shall take him into the loom.' But Summers was a young man of unusual ability. E. H. Barker, the classical scholar, who visited him in 1829 in search of information about Porson, found him 'shrewd, sensible and intelligent'; he was then in his eightieth year, in good health, and willing to talk about the remarkable boy who had come to his school sixty years before.

Under Summers, Porson learned mathematics and the rudiments of Latin; he also learned to write, and rapidly acquired a remarkable skill in penmanship. A fair-copy book of his that survives in the library of Trinity College attests not only his mathematical knowledge, but also the extraordinary neatness of his handwriting. The titles of the different sections, written with many flourishes after the manner of the professional scribe, are: Geography, Great Circle Sailing, Astronomy, Astronomical problems after the Copernic system, Variation of the compass by an Amplitude, Variation of the compass by an Azimuth, To find the moon's age, etc. Under each of these headings are a number of problems, worked out with geometrical and astronomical diagrams. Some of these problems fix the date of the book as Porson's eleventh year: 'On the 17th of August 1770 I demand the Time of the Sun's rising and setting and the length of the Day and Night at Happisburgh, the Latitude being 52 30.' 'I demand the Moon's Age, Golden Number and Epact for Oct. 25th 1770.' 'Suppose an E. and W. moon make a full sea at Hasbrow (Happisburgh spelt as pronounced) on the Full and Change Days I demand the Time of Highwater on the 25th October 1770.' With problems such as these,

1-2

many of them of a nautical character suited to a village by the sea, Richard Porson occupied his childhood.

It is surprising enough to find a scholar springing from a poor cottage in an obscure Norfolk village, but it is equally surprising to see with what ease he attained to his scholarship. Without struggles or hardship he obtained the best education in the country. That this could be so was due to the willingness of the eighteenth-century gentry to encourage and support learning, and in particular to the sympathy and generosity of the Rev. Thomas Hewitt and Mr John Norris. The former of these two gentlemen was the vicar of East Ruston. He would naturally be interested in the family of his parish clerk, especially if, as one account has it, Mrs Porson had been in service with him. He was educating his own five sons at home, and offered to instruct Richard Porson with them free of charge. Accordingly the boy, now eleven years old, left the school at Happis-burgh, and went to study under Mr Hewitt. The vicar's house was some way off at Bacton, and Porson used to spend from Monday to Saturday there, returning home for the week-ends.

For almost two years this arrangement was continued, and Mr Hewitt was so well pleased with his pupil's progress that he determined if possible to do more for him. At Witton Park, a few miles distant, lived Mr Norris, a wealthy man and disposed to exercise his benevolence in the encouragement of learning, as is shown by his foundation of a professorship of divinity at Cambridge. It might be expected that he would assist the young Porson, and Mr Hewitt therefore introduced his charge to him. Norris was not immediately impressed. 'Well,' he said, 'I see nothing particular

[4]

in this heavy-looking boy, but I confide in your account of his talents.' However, he would not commit himself, suspecting that the vicar's opinion of his pupil might be too high; not being a classical scholar himself, he consulted another clerical friend, the Rev. Thomas Carthew of Woodbridge. But Mr Carthew also did not feel himself qualified to judge, and decided to consult no less a person than the Rev. James Lambert, a friend of his, who had recently been appointed professor of Greek at Cambridge. Lambert was sympathetic and promised his help if he thought the boy deserved it. It was decided to send him to Cambridge to be examined by the professor in person. He could already write Latin hexameters, and a specimen of his work was sent before him. Lambert criticised 'fecit divina manus nos' as a rendering of 'The hand that made us is divine', but on the whole the boy was thought to have done very well. However, Carthew writing to Lambert added a warning postscript: 'You will find the lad rather an unwinning cub than otherwise, but you will I doubt not make allowances for the awkwardness of his manners.'[1]

In March 1773 the unwinning cub arrived at Cambridge, bearing with him a letter from Mr Hewitt; it told how the 'orderly and good boy' had been under his care for almost two years, and had read Erasmus's *Colloquies*, and Caesar's *Commentaries* (retranslating them into Latin), Ovid's *Metamorphoses*, all Terence, the *Eclogues*, the *Georgics*, and some of the *Aeneid*. In mathematics he was well advanced, but in Greek he was only learning the verbs. The boy was introduced to some of the Fellows of Trinity, whom he was later to meet on

[1] *Correspondence of Porson*, p. 129.

[5]

different terms. He was examined by Postlethwaite and Collier, the senior tutors, and by Atwood, a mathematician and assistant tutor. They all expressed themselves satisfied with him, and an encouraging report was sent to his patrons in Norfolk. The original scheme had been to procure for Porson a place at the Charterhouse, and Lambert applied to two of the governors of the school, but found that they had already promised their interest elsewhere. Carthew had suggested Eton if Charterhouse proved impossible, and this scheme evidently commended itself to Norris. He set about collecting subscriptions from the clergy and gentry of his acquaintance, until he had established a considerable fund, the treasurer of which was Sir George Baker, President of the College of Physicians. However, it was not until August 1774, when he was in his fifteenth year, that Porson entered Eton. The intervening period of more than a year he occupied with further study under Mr Hewitt.

Porson was at Eton on the foundation for about three and a half years. The period he spent there does not seem to have been marked by any great intellectual progress. He was not always in good health, and was not inclined to take school exercises very seriously. In a curious sentence Kidd tells us that 'about this time R.P. was prone to a spirit of intolerance, which often discomposed his nights'.[1] It is a mysterious remark, and it is not clear whether his intolerance produced a similar spirit in others which resulted in discomfort to himself, or whether it was merely his own reflections on his fellow Etonians that kept him awake at night. It may perhaps be taken as indicating a somewhat

[1] *Imperfect Outline*, p. xiii.

rebellious disposition, and even without this obscure reference we should be justified in assuming that Porson was as indifferent to success at school as he was in later life.

As to his scholarly attainments we have the testimony of a schoolfellow and friend of his, Joseph Goodall, later Headmaster and Provost of Eton. In giving evidence before a committee of the House of Commons in 1818 he was asked why Porson had not been elected to King's College. He answered that 'when he came to the school, he was placed rather higher, by the reputation of his abilities, than perhaps he ought to have been in consequence of his actual attainments.[1] With respect to prosody he knew but little; and as to Greek he had made comparatively little progress when he came to Eton. . . . In point of school exercises I think he was very inferior to more than one of his contemporaries: I would name the present Marquis Wellesley as infinitely superior to him in composition.'[2]

In fact, though he was evidently clever and well-informed, Porson's scholarship was not then considered anything out of the ordinary. 'We did not think much of the Norfolk boy', said one of his contemporaries. But he already gave evidence of unusually good memory, as is shown by an anecdote which was preserved from his school days. He was called upon one day to construe some Horace in class, and not being able to find his book borrowed his neighbour's. He proceeded to translate correctly, but apparently looking at the wrong part of the page. The master noticed this and discovered

[1] The Eton lists (ed. Austen Leigh) show Porson in the 5th form in 1775, and in the same form in 1776 and 1777. But the order of names is unaltered.

[2] Quoted by Watson, *Life of Porson*, p. 17.

[7]

that the book was Ovid's *Metamorphoses*. Porson could translate from memory without a mistake.

Even under Mr Summers Porson had given evidences of 'a little spirit of satire', and at Eton he displayed the same spirit in a lampoon on his schoolfellow, Charles Simeon, later to become famous as an evangelical leader. The lampoon, written in a disguised hand and addressed 'to the ugliest boy in Dr Davies's dominions', was brought to Simeon's notice and had the desired effect of annoying him. When the two were together at Cambridge later on, Porson did not conceal this dislike for Simeon which he had conceived at school.

Herded together in Long Chamber, without privacy, without supervision or organised occupations, the scholars of Eton found various means of amusing themselves during the long winter evenings. One of their activities was rat-hunting, which Porson once said was the only thing about Eton which he remembered with pleasure. Forty years later things were much the same, and an Etonian of that period recalled the rows of dried rat-skins that were hung up over the fire-places.[1]

Another pastime was the drama, in which Porson took part as actor and playwright. More than one of his plays were performed in Long Chamber.[2] One of them—*Out of the Frying-pan into the Fire*—is still extant. Late in life Porson repeated the play from memory to a friend, and his copy is preserved in Trinity Library. The plot is from an old legend of Friar Bacon, but in Porson's version Dr Faustus takes the place of

[1] [Tucker], *Eton of Old*, p. 54.
[2] He is also said to have acted in the private theatricals got up by Provost Barnard in the Lodge. (Forster, *Historical and Biographical Essays*, II, p. 375.)

the friar. He has conceived a scheme to build a wall of brass round Britain, in order to keep out her enemies. With the aid of Satan and Lucifer (the latter part taken by the future provost, Goodall) he gets Vulcan to make a head of brass, which is to give directions. This is placed on the fire in a frying-pan, and entrusted to the servant Punch (taken by Porson himself) and Joan his wife. They are to wait until the head speaks and then call Dr Faustus. The climax comes in the third act, when the head speaks three times. Punch and his wife are too sleepy and too much occupied with talking and singing to notice the head's remarks, and it bursts and falls into the fire, and the secret is lost. Faustus enters, and after suitably punishing his servants, delivers a soliloquy on the model of a speech of Wolsey's in *Henry VIII*, but ends by comforting himself with the reflection that England can defend herself by valour without the aid of a brazen wall.

The play is in verse, with plentiful songs, but it cannot be said that either in wit or in invention it is anything out of the ordinary. Yet Porson never forgot it, perhaps because it brought back to him the memory of a winter evening's amusement in which he was the leading spirit. There were perhaps other pleasant things about Eton besides rat-hunting. But on the whole it cannot be said that Porson looked back with any sentiment of affection or gratitude to his days at Eton, and he used to maintain that he had learnt nothing there. He did indeed acquire the Etonian's facility in Latin verse composition, as is attested by some Eton exercises of his that survive;[1] but of this pursuit he had a low opinion,

[1] There are three in Trinity College Library, and one in the British Museum (Add. MSS. 39,577).

and he did not practise it in later life. He also acknowledged that his mind was first turned to critical studies by his receiving as a prize from the headmaster a copy of Toup's *Longinus*. But it was in the congenial atmosphere of Cambridge, the University of Bentley, Dawes and Markland, that he discovered his true bent.

II

WHILE Porson was at Eton his patron Norris died, but this did not involve him in any financial difficulties, for Sir George Baker continued to exercise his benevolent interest and secured further subscribers to support the young scholar. Consequently, although not selected as scholar of King's, he could go up to Cambridge. If Provost Goodall's account of his attainments was correct, it would explain sufficiently his not proceeding to King's, but if, as seems to be the case, elections were made by seniority rather than merit, one who came to the school as late as Porson did would have small chance of being elected. So in 1778 he entered Trinity as a pensioner, and two years later he was elected scholar.

His life as an undergraduate may be assumed to have been studious and uneventful, for no record to the contrary has survived. We may assume, too, that the unwinning cub who had visited Cambridge five years before had lost much of his roughness, and that his social gifts and tastes developed. No doubt he found congenial company; Goodall, his contemporary at Eton, was at King's, and another life-long friend, Matthew Raine, was of the same year at Trinity. As for the intellectual side of Cambridge life, there was little stimulus to be obtained from the official studies of the University, or from those who taught. There were 'characters' in plenty in Cambridge; there were learned men too, and a few efficient tutors, but none of the senior residents of that period has left a name behind for intellectual eminence. There is no one who can claim the honour of having been Porson's master.

Porson pursued the obligatory studies of mathematics with sufficient success to enable him to take his degree creditably as third Senior Optime. Mathematics always interested him, but it is unlikely that he exerted himself much in this direction. He had discovered where his real interests lay. The inspiration of Bentley and Dawes led him to classical criticism, and we find him in his second year emending Theocritus and Virgil.

In 1781 he won the Craven Scholarship. The Greek iambics which he wrote on the occasion of this examination have been preserved. Though much admired at the time, they are not notably better than what a modern Craven Scholar could do, and in one respect they are worse. Three out of seventeen lines have a caesura in the fifth foot preceded by a long syllable. The rule which forbids this was formulated later by Porson himself; as an undergraduate he was unconscious of it. In the next year, soon after taking his degree, he won the first Chancellor's Medal, and was elected to a Fellowship, an exception to the then general rule at Trinity that junior Bachelors were not eligible for Fellowships.

This is perhaps the place to mention a curious story for which Maltby is the authority. 'During the earlier part of his career, he accepted the situation of tutor to a young gentleman in the Isle of Wight, but was soon forced to relinquish the office, from having been found drunk in a ditch or a turnip field.'[1] The truth of the story has been called in question, and there is no other reference to the episode, but whether true or false it illustrates a notorious characteristic of Porson: his

[1] Maltby, *Porsoniana*, p. 296.

inordinate love of drink. When he began to form his regrettable habits we do not know, but it may reasonably be supposed that they date from undergraduate days, or at least from his Fellowship. In popular imagination the eighteenth-century don is associated with heavy drinking, and the tradition is not unfounded. One might well suppose that what scandalised the Isle of Wight passed unnoticed in the combination room of Trinity.

The numerous activities, administrative and tutorial, of the present-day don were almost unknown to eighteenth-century Cambridge, and the majority of the Fellows of colleges had very little to do. Porson's only college office, that of Sublector Secundus, which he held for the year 1784–5, was a sinecure. He was free to reside or not as he chose, and to pursue those studies to which he felt himself most drawn.

One small duty fell to his lot when he was still a Bachelor Fellow; to deliver a Latin oration on the character of Charles II. The speech is extant, and is dated May 29, 1784, the anniversary of the Restoration. According to one account it was delivered in the college hall, according to another in the chapel.[1] If the latter is true, it perhaps formed part of the college exercises, from which Bachelor Fellows were not exempt, and Porson's criticism of Charles may have been set him as a thesis to maintain against the eulogy of an opponent. Whether this is so or not, the oration may well represent his real feelings, for Porson was a Whig, and the Whigs had no great love for the Stuarts. It is a severe attack on Charles's character and conduct, and allows him no merit, not even wit or humour. Its tone may be gathered

[1] Genest, *Some Account of the English stage*, I, p. 433; Beloe, *The Sexagenarian*, II, p. 285.

from the final summing up. 'Ut breviter absolvam, antequam coronam adeptus esset, mendicus fuit; postquam adeptus esset, rex non fuit: sine dignitate sapientia aut fortitudine; sine amicitia; sine fide et amore connubiali; sine fraterna pietate, atheus vivebat, Papista moriebatur. Talis fuit Carolus Secundus.
> manibus date lilia plenis;
> purpureos spargam flores animamque tyranni
> his saltem accumulem donis.'

The reader will notice a certain English ring about Porson's latinity. An accurate classical idiom was not demanded by the occasion, nor was the speech intended for publication; but even in his published works of scholarship Porson did not cultivate a flowing and pure Ciceronianism, but rather an easy natural vigour. He doubted if it was possible to imitate accurately the ancient prose styles, and therefore deprecated attempts at idiomatic elegance. 'When we write in the Latin language,' he said, 'our style should be most unambitious; we should carefully avoid all fine words and expressions, we should use the most obvious and most simple diction; beyond this we should not aspire; if we cannot present a resemblance, let us not exhibit a caricature.'[1]

Unhampered by any duties and unconcerned for the present about a career, Porson devoted himself to the study of Greek, and began to be known in the learned world for his unusual mastery of that language. His first appearance in print was in June of 1783, when he reviewed the second part of the first volume of Schütz's *Aeschylus*. His review appeared in a short-lived periodical called *Maty's New Review*, the editor of which was one

[1] Charles Butler, *Reminiscences* (1822), I, p. 292.

of Porson's colleagues at Trinity. In an earlier number of this periodical, Maty announced that Porson was preparing a new edition of Aeschylus, and invited communications from other scholars. Gilbert Wakefield rushed in with a number of worthless notes on the *Prometheus* and the *Septem*. More valuable was the communication from David Ruhnken of Leyden, to whom Porson had written asking for any unpublished fragments discovered during his work on the Greek lexicographers, and enclosing, as a proof of his abilities, some specimen emendations. Ruhnken replied with some valuable notes, which were however not destined to be used, for the projected edition of Aeschylus was never completed.[1] The Cambridge Press was preparing to publish a second edition of Stanley's *Aeschylus*, and Porson at first undertook the editorship. But the Syndics of the Press required him to keep Stanley's text unaltered and to reprint all Pauw's notes. Porson was unable to accept these conditions. He had a low opinion of Pauw, whom he described as a 'miserable critic, in whom singular ignorance and as singular arrogance were combined';[2] and, as he later remarked, 'whatever editor...republishes a book from an old edition, when the text might be improved from subsequent discoveries, while he hopes to shew his modesty and religion, only exposes his indolence, his ignorance or his superstition'.[3]

He suffered a further rebuff when the Syndics proved unwilling to pay the expenses of a visit to Florence, where he hoped to collate the famous Medicean MS.

[1] The notes subsequently perished in the fire at Merton, see p. 59.
[2] Review of Schütz's *Aeschylus*, *Tracts and Criticisms*, p. 7.
[3] Review of Edwards's *Plutarch*, *Tracts and Criticisms*, p. 89.

of Aeschylus. 'Let Mr Porson collect his manuscripts at home', said Dr Torkington, Master of Clare and Vice-Chancellor. Porson was disappointed and gave up for the time being the project of editing Aeschylus. When writing on a different subject a few years later, he did not forget to publish the ignorance of the 'learned doctor in our University who confounded the collection with the collation of manuscripts'.[1]

We can hardly doubt that Aeschylus would have profited, and perhaps Porson too, by a visit to Florence and a collation of the best manuscript. As it was, Porson remained in this country. He celebrated in verse his potations with foreign scholars, but these potations remained imaginary:

> I went to Strasburg, where I got drunk
> With that most learn'd professor, Brunck.
> I went to Wortz, where I got more drunken
> With that more learn'd professor, Ruhnken.

The lines were circulated as Porson's, and may well belong to this period, when he was concerned with the work of both of these scholars. They have misled some to suppose that these convivial meetings actually took place.[2] In fact, Porson knew contemporary scholars of other countries only by their work and sometimes by correspondence; he never left England throughout his life.

He reviewed one or two more books for Maty before the *New Review* came to an end. The longest and most important of these contributions is his review of Brunck's *Aristophanes*, written in 1783, which contains some exhilarating criticisms of the editor's methods and

[1] *Letters to Travis*, p. 57.
[2] As Edith Sitwell in *The English Eccentrics*.

manners. Brunck had apologised for the shortcomings of his edition by attributing them to the hurry in which he wrote his notes and the interruptions of his son playing in his study and his friends who came and conversed with him at all hours of the day. 'Tantamne rem tam negligenter?' asks Porson. 'I think in such a case I should have sent Master Brunck out of the room. Pugh! says Mr B. (or I suppose would say, if he read Shakespeare) "He talks to me that never had a son." But to be serious. What right has any man to publish a work of this kind in a hurry?'[1] Porson remarks, too, on the asperity with which Brunck had treated other scholars, in particular Kuster and Bergler. 'Bergler with him is fungus, stipes, bardus, and what not. If Mr B. is better qualified than Kuster and Bergler to publish Aristophanes (as doubtless he is by far), "let him give God thanks, and make no boast of it"; but why triumph over men who are not in a condition to return the attack? Παῦε, παῦ', ὦ δέσποθ' Ἑρμῆ, μὴ λέγε· Ἀλλ' ἔα τὸν ἄνδρ' ἐκεῖνον, οὗπερ ἔστ', εἶναι κάτω.'[2]

The review is prefaced by a lucid and judicious vindication of Aristophanes against some recent criticisms, ending with the following words: 'To sum up Aristophanes's character, if we consider his just and severe ridicule of the Athenian foibles, his detestation of the expensive and ruinous war in which Greece was engaged, his pointed invectives against the factious and interested demagogues, "who bawl'd for freedom in their senseless mood"; his contempt of the useless and frivolous inquiries of the Sophists; his wit, and versatility of style; the astonishing playfulness, originality and fertility of his imagination; the great harmony of versification,

[1] Kidd, *Tracts and Criticisms*, p. 18.   [2] *Id.* p. 19.

whenever the subject required it, and his most refined elegance of language; in spite of Dr Beattie's dictum, we shall look over his blemishes, and allow that with all his faults, he might be a very good citizen, and was certainly an excellent Poet.'[1]

Minor reviews were those of Weston's *Hermesianax* and Huntingford's *Apology for the Monostrophics.* Both of these were books of a type that rarely appear to-day. Weston's was a collection of textual emendations of small merit such as would to-day be published in the classical periodicals and soon forgotten. Huntingford was a Winchester master who wrote original Greek verse with an inadequate knowledge of metre and an inability to admit his own mistakes; Porson already had a better idea of Greek prosody than most, and had little patience with one who not only wrote bad Greek verse, but also referred ignorantly and offensively to a better scholar than himself, Richard Dawes. Porson concludes his review with these words: 'Without entering on a long defence of Dawes, I shall venture to urge one plea in his favour. He wrote in youth some Greek verses, full of mistakes in syntax and dialect, *though faultless, I believe*, in point of metre. But afterwards, becoming sensible of his error, he quitted what he esteemed so idle and unprofitable a study, and chose rather to read good Greek than to write bad. An example of candour and prudence well worthy to be imitated.'[2]

Porson also published in *Maty's Review* in April 1786 some letters of Le Clerc and Bentley, with a few notes of his own; and in the same year, when Hutchinson's edition of Xenophon's *Anabasis* was being reissued, he

[1] *Tracts and Criticisms*, p. 15.   [2] *Id.* p. 52.

added a few notes to oblige Nicholson, the well-known Cambridge bookseller.

Porson was not only interested in Greek, he was also a keen critic of contemporary writing. In 1787 he brought his wit to bear on a new and inferior book, Sir John Hawkins's *Life of Johnson*. He published in *The Gentleman's Magazine* three letters of ironical eulogy, beginning thus: 'Have you read that divine book, the "Life of Samuel Johnson LL.D. by Sir John Hawkins, Knt?" Have you done anything but read it since it was first published? For my own part I scruple not to declare, that I could not rest till I had read it quite through, notes, digressions, index and all;—then I could not rest till I had gone over it a second time. I begin to think that increase of appetite grows by what it feeds on; for I have been reading it ever since. I am now in the midst of the sixteenth perusal; and still I discover new beauties.'[1] Porson continues in the same vein, and includes what he claims is a missing page of the book, and is in fact Porson's own parody of Hawkins's style. The book is now forgotten except by Johnsonian students, but Porson's letters on it may still be read with amusement. The parody has been described as 'of startling excellence', and the whole performance as 'executed in the best manner of Swift'.[2] It is no surprise when we read that Porson knew and admired Swift's works.

Apart from his literary work there is not much to be said about the period of Porson's Fellowship at Trinity. He does not seem to have resided regularly at Cambridge.

[1] *Tracts and Criticisms*, p. 333.
[2] Oliver Elton, *Survey of English Literature*, 1780–1830, ii, p. 380.

It appears from a letter of 1784 that he had already taken the rooms in the Temple (5 Essex Court) that he occupied in later life. In December 1789 he writes to a friend at Trinity asking him to receive his dividend from the bursar and send it to London, and, being doubtful whether he will come to Cambridge that winter, asks for the latest news of college affairs.[1] And on February 3 of the next year he asks the same friend to consult a manuscript in the Trinity College Library, remarking that he hopes to come to Cambridge shortly.[2] On the 23rd he is still in London.[3] Evidently he had already acquired the dislike of moving that was later a notorious characteristic.

Sometimes he visited Goodall at Eton; he was there in 1789 finishing the *Letters to Travis* and arranging for their publication. Nearly three months of 1790 he spent with Dr Parr at Hatton. The Rev. Samuel Parr, LL.D., though now almost forgotten, was in his day a considerable figure. He combined Whig principles with Johnsonian diction and mannerisms; his pipe and his wig were scarcely less famous than his extensive learning and his Latin epitaphs. At this time he was curate of Hatton in Warwickshire, where he took pupils and acquired a library which eventually numbered 10,000 volumes.

Parr had a great admiration for Porson, but his admiration was not reciprocated. Porson delighted in exercising his wit against the pompous doctor. 'Porson hated me', wrote Parr in a letter of his testy old age, '...and at the midnight meetings of College boys and ale-house cellar sots he very often was witty upon

[1] *Correspondence*, p. 29.   [2] *Id.* p. 30.
[3] *Id.* p. 48.

Dr Bellenden'[1]—a nickname for Parr derived from the *Preface to Bellendenus*, his most famous work. In Parr's presence Porson was no more respectful. On one occasion the doctor attempted to draw him into a philosophical discussion. 'Pray, Mr Porson, what do you think of the introduction of moral and physical evil into the world?' 'Why, doctor,' answered Porson, 'I think we should have done very well without it.' Parr was a character who invited such treatment and too seldom got it, but it is to his credit that in spite of it he continued friendly to Porson, did his best to help him, and often expressed his high opinion of his abilities.[2]

In 1789 we find Parr worrying about Porson's future. 'Where is Porson?' he writes to Burney,[3] a common friend of the two. 'And how does he relish the new Master of Trinity? For heaven's sake rouse him to write some book—to fix upon some profession—to secure some independence. Dum quid sit, dubitat, life runs away, and yet the rogue loves good port, and good tobacco, and when with you he can appease his genius with good claret and good Madeira,—all good things, I say; but better non deficiente crumena.'[4] For some years Parr had been hoping to have Porson with him at Hatton, and in 1790 he eventually arrived there, and stayed for a considerable time. Parr's biographer, Johnstone, describes how he would rise late and spend most of the day reading in the library. 'At night, when he could collect the young men of the family together, and especially if Parr was absent from home, he was

---

[1] Letter to Butler in Butler's *Life of Samuel Butler*, I, p. 144.
[2] See Parr's *Works*, VII, p. 407.
[3] Charles Burney, son of the historian of music and sister of Fanny (Madame D'Arblay).   [4] Parr's *Works*, VII, p. 411.

in his glory. The charms of his society were irresistible. Many a midnight hour did I spend with him, listening with delight while he poured out torrents of various literature, the best sentences of the best writers, and sometimes the ludicrous beyond the gay; pages of Barrow, whole letters of Richardson, whole scenes of Foote; favourite pieces from the periodical press, and, among them, I have heard recited the "Orgies of Bacchus".[1]

The visit came to an end when Mrs Parr could no longer tolerate Porson's habits, and showed her disapproval by a designed insult. Parr's biographer refrains from describing the nature of the insult, but tradition says that she substituted a close-stool for Porson's chair at table.[2]

[1] Parr's *Works*, I, p. 379. Johnstone's memory has played him false. The *Orgies of Bacchus* were not written till 1793.

[2] Butler, *Life of Samuel Butler*, I, p. 57.

III

Porson's most important literary work of this period, the *Letters to Travis*, has so far been barely mentioned; something more must now be said about this, his only excursion into sacred criticism. In 1781 appeared the third volume of the *Decline and Fall*. In the 37th chapter Gibbon, writing of the frauds used by orthodox theologians to confound the Arians, instanced the interpolated verse in the first Epistle of St John (ch. v, v. 7) which concerns the Three Heavenly Witnesses. 'The memorable text,' wrote Gibbon, 'which asserts the unity of the THREE who bear witness in heaven, is condemned by the universal silence of the orthodox fathers, ancient versions, and authentic manuscripts. It was first alleged by the Catholic bishops whom Hunneric summoned to the conference of Carthage. An allegorical interpretation, in the form, perhaps, of a marginal note, invaded the text of the Latin Bibles, which were renewed and corrected in a dark period of ten centuries. After the invention of printing, the editors of the Greek Testament yielded to their own prejudices, or those of the times; and the pious fraud, which was embraced with equal zeal at Rome and at Geneva, has been infinitely multiplied in every country and every language of modern Europe.'

The verse had been condemned by scholars before Gibbon; in England its opponents had included Newton and Bentley, the latter of whom made it the subject of his praelection as Divinity professor in 1717. This dissertation was not printed and is no longer extant, though it was known to Porson. But the critics had had little influence, and, whether through ignorance or through a desire to preserve a text that gave scriptural support to the doctrine of the Trinity, divines continued to quote the Three Heavenly Witnesses as genuine Scripture.

Gibbon's remarks aroused the Rev. George Travis, archdeacon of Chester, to come forward as champion of the verse. His letters to Gibbon first appeared in *The Gentleman's Magazine* for 1782, and were afterwards reprinted with additions in 1784, and again with further additions a few years later. Travis was an ignorant man, and had read little on his subject apart from a defence of the verse by a French pastor called Martin, whom (in translation) he followed closely, adding some errors of his own. But in spite of this his book was read widely and convinced a number of readers. Porson had read Gibbon's volume and Travis's letters and had formed his opinion of the archdeacon's case. He was hindered for a time, he says, by his natural indolence, his engagement in other studies, and his contempt for Travis's work, but an anonymous challenge to Gibbon in *The Gentleman's Magazine* inspired him to appear in print. In 1788 and 1789 he published seven letters to Archdeacon Travis in *The Gentleman's Magazine*, which were afterwards reprinted with much additional matter in a book of over four hundred pages.

'The wretched Travis still howls under the lash of the merciless Porson', wrote Gibbon in his *Autobiography*.[1] Porson's letters might have been expected to end the controversy, but some still remained uncon-

[1] (Ed. 1896), p. 323.

vinced. It is not easy to say the last word in a matter like this. After Bentley's *Dissertation* there were still those who believed in the *Epistles of Phalaris*; and the *Letters to Travis* did not prevent some from continuing to believe in the Three Heavenly Witnesses. In particular, Bishop Burgess of Salisbury renewed the defence of the text after Porson's death, and was answered by Turton, later bishop of Ely, in his *Vindication of the Literary character of Professor Porson*. But the subsequent history of the controversy does not concern us. If Porson did not end it, it was not the fault of his *Letters*.

Gibbon, not in this case a wholly disinterested judge, commended them as 'the most acute and accurate piece of criticism which has appeared since the days of Bentley'.[1] 'Porson's strictures', he added, 'are founded in argument, enriched with learning and enlivened with wit, and his adversary neither deserves nor finds any quarter at his hands.'

The wit commended by Gibbon, which in places approaches flippancy, has given offence to some readers, and Porson himself anticipated the objection that he had 'treated a grave subject with too much levity, and a dignitary of the church with too much freedom'.[2] To this he answered that 'to peruse such a mass of falsehood and sophistry without sometimes giving way to laughter was to me at least impossible' and that 'by reading Mr Travis I have been insensibly infected with his spirit'. The modern reader (if there are any such) will not regret these impertinences that enliven occasionally the controversial pages. 'At last up starts a grave and reverend gentleman and tells us with a serious face that it is not day at noon. And this trash we are expected

[1] *Autobiography*, p. 323.   [2] *Letters to Travis*, p. xxii.

to refute, or the Mumpsimus regiment will boast here-
after that we have not accepted their leader's challenge.'[1]
'A ray of light however pierced the Egyptian darkness
of your mind.'[2] Or this conclusion to the discussion of
the supposed MSS. of Stephanus and Beza containing
the disputed verse: 'I am compelled to decide (with
sorrow I pronounce it!) that they have disappeared;
perhaps they were too good for this world, and therefore
are no longer visible on earth. However, I advise the
true believers not to be dejected; for since all things
lost from earth are treasured up in the lunar sphere,
they may rest assured, that these valuable relics are
safely deposited in a snug corner of the moon, fit company for Constantine's donation, Orlando's wits and
Mr Travis's learning.'[3]

These are some specimens of Porson in his most
youthful and irrepressible mood. Occasionally we hear
a sterner note. 'Mankind are in general so lazy and
credulous, that when once they are prejudiced in favour
of any person's veracity, they will regard another as
a calumniator who endeavours to convince them that
they have bestowed their approbation upon an unworthy
object.'[4] 'But in truth, it is much easier and pleasanter
to go on believing everything that we hear or read,
than to undergo the labour of enquiry or the pain of
suspense.'[5]

Porson owed something to Bentley, whose *Phalaris*
he, of course, knew, and once or twice he pays him the
compliment of verbal allusion. Quotations from Swift
suggest a further affinity. Indeed a peculiar feature of
Porson's style is the number of quotations included in

[1] *Letters to Travis*, p. 60.   [2] *Id.* p. 66.
[3] *Id.* p. 87.   [4] *Id.* p. 170.   [5] *Id.* p. 338.

the text, without any words of introduction; lines from poetry, sentences from prose authors he had read, Latin, English and French, stuck in his mind, and came out unsought as he wrote. He is also apt to indulge that tendency to irony and allusiveness that was always a feature of his writing, and which sometimes misled the unwary; indeed there was some excuse for not realising that when he spoke of being 'extremely fond of Gregory Nazianzen',[1] he did not mean what he said, but was only alluding to a Cambridge joke of his day.[2]

The *Letters to Travis* is a controversial work, not a critical dissertation; it was aimed at confuting Archdeacon Travis, and owes its form to its occasion. An independent work of criticism would have been less diffuse, perhaps less amusing; but without Mr Travis Porson would most probably not have written at all on this subject. It was the desire to expose the ignorance and disingenuousness of the archdeacon that led Porson to write, rather than any great interest in New Testament studies for their own sake. His strong love of truth made him undertake the task and execute it thoroughly and conscientiously, but he never returned to theological studies, and is said to have regretted the time spent

[1] *Letters to Travis*, p. 223; cf. p. 272 'my favourite Gregory'.
[2] The story is thus given by Luard (*Cambridge Essays*, 1857, p. 141 n.): 'Bp. Watson one day before presiding at an act, as Regius Professor of Divinity, in the schools, was overtaken by a friend out riding, who mentioned that there was a passage of Gregory Nazianzen of singular fitness for the morrow's disputation. "Is there?" said Watson. "I never read a word of him." "Never mind," the other replied, "I will send you my copy with the leaf turned down at the passage." The next day the Professor came out glibly with the extract, ending it with "Haec ex Gregorio illo Nazianzeno, quem semper in deliciis habui."'

on them. He did not make or point the way to any advance in New Testament criticism, which had languished since Bentley and had to wait until Lachmann for further stimulus.

Porson anticipated the charge of heresy that was likely to be brought against one who attacked the famous Trinitarian text. He answered that 'he does the best service to truth, who hinders it from being supported by falsehood',[1] and attacked that 'spurious orthodoxy, which is the overflowing of zeal without knowledge... which whenever a rotten and ruinous outwork of religion is demolished, utters as hideous a shriek as if the very foundations of the Church of Christ nodded to her fall'.[2] This is well enough, but the disrespectful way in which the fathers and even the apostles are treated in the letters might well lead to suspicions as to the author's religious sympathies. Porson was credited with Socinianism by some as a result of the book, and the information that he had written 'against Christianity' led an old friend and supporter of his, Mrs Turner of Norwich, to cut down her intended legacy to him from £300 to £30.

The chapter began with Gibbon and may fitly end with him. The best-known piece of the *Letters to Travis* is that part of the Preface which contains Porson's criticisms of the *Decline and Fall*. There is no doubt about Porson's admiration for Gibbon's work, which he regarded as the greatest literary production of the century, but, as Gibbon put it, 'the sweetness of his praise is tempered by a reasonable admixture of acid'.[3] The passage has often been quoted in part, but it is so

[1] *Letters to Travis*, p. xxv. [2] *Id.* p. xxvi.
[3] *Autobiography*, p. 338.

characteristic and so acute that it deserves to be reproduced in full.[1]

'An impartial judge, I think, must allow that Mr Gibbon's History is one of the ablest performances of its kind that has ever appeared. His industry is indefatigable; his accuracy scrupulous; his reading, which indeed is sometimes ostentatiously displayed, immense; his attention always awake; his memory retentive; his style emphatic and expressive; his periods harmonious. His reflections are often just and profound; he pleads eloquently for the rights of mankind, and the duty of toleration; nor does his humanity ever slumber except when women are ravished,[2] or the Christians persecuted.[3]

'Though his style is in general correct and elegant, he sometimes *draws out the thread of his verbosity finer than the staple of his argument*.[4] In endeavouring to avoid vulgar terms he too frequently dignifies trifles, and clothes common thoughts in a splendid dress that would be rich enough for the noblest ideas. In short, we are too often reminded of that *great man*, Mr Prig, *the auctioneer*, whose manner was so inimitably fine that he had as much to say on a ribbon as a Raphael.[5]

'Sometimes, in his anxiety to vary his phrase, he becomes obscure; and, instead of calling his personages by their names, defines them by their birth, alliance, office, or other circumstances of their history. Thus an honest gentleman is often described by a circumlocution, lest the same word should be twice repeated in the same page. Sometimes epithets are added which the tenor of the sentence renders unnecessary. Sometimes, in his

[1] *Letters to Travis*, p. xxviii. The notes are those of Porson.
[2] Chap. LVII, note 54.   [3] See the whole of chap. XVI.
[4] *Love's Labour's Lost*.   [5] Foote's *Minor*.

[29]

attempts at elegance, he loses sight of English, and sometimes of sense.

'A less pardonable fault is the rage for indecency which pervades the whole work, but especially the last volumes. And, to the honour of his consistency, this is the same man who is so prudish that he dares not call Belisarius a cuckold, because it is too bad a word for a *decent* historian to use. If the history were anonymous, I should guess that these disgraceful obscenities were written by some *débauché*, who, having from age, or accident, or excess, survived the practice of lust, still indulged himself in the luxury of speculation; and exposed the impotent imbecility, after he had lost the vigour of the passions.[1]

'But these few faults make no considerable abatement in my general esteem. Notwithstanding all its particular defects, I greatly admire the whole; as I should admire a beautiful face in the author, though it were tarnished with a few freckles; or as I should admire an elegant person and address, though they were blemished with a little affectation.'

Not long after the publication of the *Letters to Travis*, Gibbon invited his champion and critic to call on him, and thanked him for his work. But the interview did not result in a closer acquaintance. Apart from a certain similarity of interests and sympathies there was little to draw the two men together. There was a primness about Gibbon which does not seem to accord well with Porson's caustic sincerity. So far as we know the two did not meet again.

[1] Junius.

Note in HOMERVM.

31

Od. Π. 294. Repetit infra, T. 13. Transtulerunt Val. Flacc. Argonaut. V. 541. Tertullian. de Pall. IV. p. 18. 47. ed.
Salmaf. 1656. parodii expressit Juvenal. IX. 37.   [Soph. El. 1244.
IA. Z. 484. Hinc colorem sumpsere Longus Pastoral. I. p. 26. et Valer. Flaccus Argonaut. VII. 215. cf. Long. II. p. so
B. 315. Huc forsan respexerunt nitidissimi scriptores Moschus Idyl. IV. 21. Heliodorus Æthiopic. II. p. 97.
H. 92. Non abludit illud Livii VII. 10.
Z. 429. Huic loco sua debent Ovid. Heroid. III. 51. Val. Flacc. Argonaut. III. 323.

MENT AN. Aristoph. Acharn. 161. 543.   *Jasitheus*   *Jasitheus*   *stcio and secus*
ΦΕΥΞΟΜΑΙ. 202. 1128.

JASITHEVS   *Jasitheus*   *Jasitheus*

Jasitheus al. Raphael Fabretti

[Greek and cursive lines]

ας εγω και ΔΙΓΟΥΗ ιγκηδω ρηρτινα, ΙοΓιςκουε
Ετ σοροp ετ κοφνιυτξ, ανος κημ γεντετοτ ανυος

Γ. αις   αι^{w}-   αιυ.

αρεω

Ast ego quæ Dworom invicto reg .   αχιυ.

x

ξκιι ζαι?

.

IV

THE statutes of Trinity required that Fellows of the college should be in holy orders by the time seven years had elapsed from their taking of the M.A. degree. Porson's period of grace elapsed in 1792, and it had been known for a year or two that he had no intention of being ordained. There were however two Fellowships open to laymen. As one of these was vacant, Porson applied for it, and had every ground for expecting to succeed to it, since Dr Postlethwaite, the Master of Trinity, had apparently promised it to him. But the Master changed his mind, and gave the lay Fellowship to a relative of his own, writing meanwhile to Porson with the suggestion that he should keep his Fellowship by taking orders.

The doctor may have been under the impression that Porson was willing to be ordained, like most Fellows of colleges, as a matter of course. Or being a staunch defender of the Establishment, he may have wished to be rid of a Fellow of suspected orthodoxy.[1] Whatever his motives his conduct appears to have been reprehensible. Porson certainly felt that he had been unfairly treated, and his friends agreed with him. 'You have done me every injury in your power', he told Postlethwaite, when he met him in London. It was an interview which cannot have been pleasant for the Master; he

[1] A third but less likely reason which was current later was that Postlethwaite had feared that Porson's frequent intoxication might be a bad example to the young. (Pryme, *Autobiographic Recollections*, p. 85.)

[31]

had gone to London to elect the Westminster scholars, and Porson called on him at the school. Postlethwaite was trembling all over, and had to support himself by the pillar near him. In later life Porson would describe the interview to his friends, and tell how at the end of it Postlethwaite said not a word, but burst into tears and left the room.[1]

To vacate a Fellowship through unwillingness to take orders was an unusual thing in eighteenth-century Cambridge, where the standard of piety and morality required of academic clergy was not very exacting.[2] It was a courageous thing, too, for outside the church there was small chance for a classical scholar to make a living. Something could be earned by publishing editions or by correcting works for the press; Porson himself did some work of this sort, as when he saw through the press an English edition of Heyne's *Virgil*. But scholars who hoped to make a living by literary enterprises, like E. H. Barker a generation or so later, might find themselves in the debtor's prison. As Fellow, Porson had latterly received on an average about £75 a year.[3] It is commonly stated that after vacating his Fellowship he lived for a time in poverty. But by the end of the year he had, as we shall see, new means of support, and the Bursar's Books of Trinity show that he received

---

[1] I assume that the letter of Hughes quoted on p. 79 refers to the same occasion, though there the interview is said to have been in Porson's chambers.

[2] Robert Tyrwhitt of Jesus, the Unitarian, and Henry Homer of Emmanuel, the classical scholar, had resigned their Fellowships for reasons of conscience, the former in 1777, the latter in 1788. Tyrwhitt was already in priest's and Homer in deacon's orders.

[3] As Bachelor Fellow he had received about £30 a year.

a dividend for the year 1792–3 as well as for the previous year. It is difficult to find a place for that period of poverty during which, we are told, he was reduced to living for a month on a guinea.[1] But of course when he decided not to take orders he had no certainty of a future livelihood.

He was much downcast when his Fellowship expired, and we are told that he shed tears and 'recited with inexpressible fervour and solemnity the third chapter of Job'.[2] It may seem to show a certain lack of proportion to compare the afflictions of Job with the academic slight administered by Dr Postlethwaite, but it was not only the prospect of poverty that distressed Porson, it was also the sense of being an outcast from his University. In spite of appearances to the contrary, he must have had a high sense of the dignity of his profession, and a strong desire to advance classical scholarship. What he regarded (with some justice) as his expulsion from Cambridge was a heavy blow not only to himself but also to learning.

His friends in London were anxious to show that they at any rate appreciated his merits, and even before the Fellowship was actually vacated subscriptions were being obtained towards the purchasing of an annuity for him. It was to be 'a tribute of literary men to literature, which had been deserted by the University, or rather by its own college'. So wrote Dr Raine, a close friend of Porson and one of the chief promoters of the scheme, to Parr, urging at the same time the impropriety of applying to the Master of Trinity.[3]

---

[1] Other accounts give the period as three weeks and six weeks.
[2] Kidd, *Imperfect Outline*, p. xxix.
[3] Parr's *Works*, VII, p. 528.

CRP

[33]

3

It is worth while perhaps to call attention to the phrase 'a tribute to literature'. The classical scholar in the eighteenth century had a place in the literary world by virtue of his classical scholarship. There was no estrangement or rivalry between different branches of learning, nor between learning and literature. The enmity between classical learning and scientific or economic studies belonged to the age of Brougham rather than to that of Fox, and the literary man's dislike for the learned, as expressed by Hazlitt in a famous essay, was a product of the romantic movement yet to come. Thus a wide circle, including some who did not altogether share Porson's interests, were ready to show their respect for classical learning by subscribing to the fund.

By the end of the year the total amount was getting near £2000, and it was possible to purchase for Porson an annuity of £100. He accepted it on condition that the principal should return to the donors at his death. When he died those of the donors who were still alive used the money to found the prize and scholarship at Cambridge which now bear his name.[1]

Before the collection of subscriptions was concluded Porson had obtained a new position at Cambridge. In July of 1792 his Fellowship lapsed, and in October of the same year the professorship of Greek became vacant. The Regius professorship of Greek, founded by Henry VIII, had by the eighteenth century become an office of small importance; its salary remained at its original figure of £40, and no professor had lectured since the previous century. The seven electors included

[1] The Porson Prize for Greek iambics was founded in 1816. The remaining money was left to accumulate for the founding of a scholarship. The first Porson Scholar was elected in 1855.

the Master and the two senior Fellows of Trinity, and consequently the appointment usually went to a member of that college. 'The chair had come to be regarded as a sinecure of trifling value to which Fellows of Trinity had the first claim, and consequently most of its occupants during the eighteenth century were entirely undistinguished.'[1] Lambert, whom we have met already as examiner of the young Porson, had been succeeded by William Cooke, who was an exception to the general rule in being a Fellow of King's, but no exception in his lack of distinction. His retirement had for some years been expected, and Porson, hoping to succeed, had planned to restore the prestige of the chair by giving lectures.

When Cooke's resignation took place, the Master of Trinity at once wrote to Porson, suggesting that he should apply. Postlethwaite was evidently trying to make amends for the wrong he had done. But Porson was little inclined to respond to the Master's overtures. He felt himself an outcast from Cambridge and had resolved to have no further connection with the University. Moreover, he was under the impression that subscription was required of a professor—subscription, that is, to the Prayer Book and Articles and the Royal Supremacy—and this his conscience and his pride forbade him to undergo. His rather bitter letter to Postlethwaite has been preserved.

Sir,—When I first received the favour of your letter, I must own that I felt rather vexation and chagrin than hope and satisfaction. I had looked upon myself so completely in the light of an outcast from Alma Mater, that I had made up my mind to have no further connection with the place. The

---

[1] Winstanley, *Unreformed Cambridge*, p. 119.

prospect you held out to me gave me more uneasiness than pleasure. When I was younger than I now am, and my disposition more sanguine than it is at present, I was in daily expectation of Mr Cooke's resignation, and I flattered myself with the hope of succeeding to the honour he was going to quit. As hope and ambition are great castle-builders, I had laid a scheme, partly, as I was willing to think, for the joint credit, partly for the mutual advantage, of myself and the University. I had projected a plan of reading lectures, and I persuaded myself that I should easily obtain a grace permitting me to exact a certain sum from every person who attended. But seven years' waiting will tire out the most patient temper; and all my ambition of this sort was long ago laid asleep. The sudden news of the vacant professorship put me in mind of poor Jacob, who having served seven years in hopes of being rewarded with Rachel, awoke, and behold it was Leah.

Such, Sir, I confess, were the first ideas that took possession of my mind. But after a little reflection, I resolved to refer a matter of this importance to my friends. This circumstance has caused the delay, for which I ought before now to have apologised. My friends unanimously exhorted me to embrace the good fortune which they conceived to be in my grasp. Their advice, therefore, joined to the expectation I had entertained of doing some small good by my exertions in the employment, together with the pardonable vanity which the honour annexed to the office inspired, determined me; and I was on the point of troubling you, Sir, and the other electors, with notice of my intentions to profess myself a candidate, when an objection, which had escaped me in the hurry of my thoughts, now occurred to my recollection.

The same reason which hindered me from keeping my fellowship by the method you obligingly pointed out to me, would, I am greatly afraid, prevent me from being Greek Professor. Whatever concern this may give me for myself, it gives me none for the public. I trust there are at least twenty or thirty in the University equally able and willing to undertake the office; possessed, many of talents superior to mine, and all of a more complying conscience. This I speak upon the supposition that the next Greek professor will be compelled to read lectures; but if the place remains a sinecure, the number of qualified persons will be greatly increased. And though it were even granted that my industry and attention might possibly produce some benefit to the interests of learning and the credit of the University, that trifling gain would be as much exceeded by keeping the professorship a sinecure, and bestowing it on a sound believer, as temporal considerations are outweighed by spiritual. Having only a strong persuasion, not an absolute certainty, that such a subscription is required of the professor elect, if I am mistaken, I hereby offer myself as a candidate; but if I am right in my opinion, I shall beg of you to order my name to be erased from the boards, and I shall esteem it a favour conferred on, Sir,

Your obliged humble servant,

R. PORSON.[1]

Ignoring Porson's irony, Postlethwaite hastened to assure him that subscription was not necessary. The Act of Uniformity of 1662 required professors to declare that they would conform to the liturgy of the Church of England, but this was of little relevance to a layman. The University imposed no subscription in addition to what it demanded on the taking of degrees. Porson had presumably subscribed on taking his M.A., and must have discovered his scruples since then. After receiving Postlethwaite's assurances he consented to become a candidate, and was unanimously elected on November 1, 1792. Cambridge had not had a layman as Greek professor since the sixteenth century, and was to wait until Jebb for another.

[1] *Correspondence,*p. 49.

As candidate for the professorship, Porson was obliged by statute to undergo an examination; this was a mere formality, except for the praelection, an institution which lasted until recent years. The subject of his lecture, which was delivered before the electors and the general public, was his favourite Greek author, Euripides; it was in Latin, according to custom, and was composed in two days only. Hastily written as it was, we may be grateful that it was preserved, if only because of the limitations it reveals. The great textual critics of the past were not ready to discuss in general terms the authors whose texts they studied with such minute care, and when one does so his criticism has a special interest. It must be admitted that Porson's criticism is not particularly illuminating; Wilamowitz even went so far as to say that 'in the face of such a trivial discussion of the poetry of Euripides and the merits of the *Hecuba* the reader will rejoice that the great master of language never except here went outside the bounds of the linguistic'.[1]

The major part of the praelection is occupied with a discussion of the *Hecuba*, but this is preceded by some general observations on the merits and faults of Euripides, and a comparison of him with the other two tragedians. Between Sophocles and Euripides he sums up as follows: 'Interea non diffiteor maiorem me quidem voluptatem ex Euripidis nativa venustate et inaffectata simplicitate percipere quam ex magis elaborata et artificiosa Sophoclis sedulitate. Hic fortasse meliores tragoedias scripsit; sed ille dulciora poemata. Hunc magis probare solemus; illum magis amare; hunc laudamus; illum legimus.'[2] We may disagree with Porson's judg-

---

[1] *Herakles*, I, p. 230.
[2] *Adversaria*, p. 11.

[38]

ment or think his outlook limited, but we cannot fail to admire the precision and neatness of his expression. We are reminded of Quintilian, but Porson needed no model to teach him a crisp and lucid style, whether in Latin or English.

When he took up the professorship, Porson intended to break with recent tradition and deliver lectures, but for some reason he never did so. In some accounts it is stated that the University authorities discouraged him by not allowing him rooms to lecture in, but this story does not proceed from the best informed sources and we cannot be sure that it is correct.[1] It is recorded that Porson himself, when asked why he did not lecture, answered 'Because I thought better on it. Whatever originality my lectures might have had, people would have cried out, "We knew all this before."'[2] Which sounds rather like an excuse for laziness or disinclination.

About this time, talking of the Greek professorship, he complained to a friend of 'the difficulty of recalling the mind to a pursuit from which it has been torn; and how hard a task it was when a man's spirit has once been broken to renovate it'.[3] He was still in depressed mood, and unwilling to forget his grudge against Cambridge; and perhaps he was becoming too accustomed to life in London to be willing to start as a lecturer in Cambridge. He was also, as we shall see in the next chapter, engaged with new and unacademic interests. At this time he was

[1] Pryse Gordon says Porson actually began to give lectures, but he admits that he knows little of Porson's life at Cambridge. *Personal Memoirs*, I, p. 287.

[2] Maltby, *Porsoniana*, p. 312.

[3] Letter from Burney to Parr, Parr's *Works*, VII, p. 413.

more of a Londoner than a Cambridge man. But his new office was not completely a sinecure; the professor of Greek had to examine for the Craven Scholarships and Chancellor's Medals, and for this purpose Porson would visit Cambridge annually, and spend some time in residence at Trinity. But for the greater part of the year he lived in London, in his chambers in Essex Court.

V

I N his Cambridge praelection, Porson had made a passing reference to current events,[1] which serves to remind us that in 1792 there were other things to interest Cambridge beside the election of a new Greek professor. Englishmen had been watching with various feelings the progress of the French Revolution, though the September massacres of that year converted many of those who had at first been favourable to the French Republic. The University, no less than the rest of the country, was anxious to repudiate any suspicion of disloyalty or Jacobinism. That winter in Cambridge 'Church and King' mobs paraded the streets, and Tom Paine was burnt in effigy on Market Hill.[2]

Porson was far from indifferent to politics. We hear of him visiting the House of Commons in 1792 to hear the debates on the Birmingham riots,[3] and he was by way of being a judge of political oratory. His remark on Fox has often been quoted: 'Mr Pitt conceives his sentences before he utters them. Mr Fox throws himself into the middle of his, and leaves it to God almighty to get him out again.' Porson's sympathies were on the side of reform. He was in favour of the French Revolution, at any rate in its beginnings, and in home politics remained opposed to Pitt's government. He was on

[1] 'Regerit Euripides, quod forsan ad res, quae hodie geruntur, detorquere quis posset, μὰ τὸν 'Απόλλω, Δημοκρατικὸν γὰρ αὖτ' ἔδρων.' *Adversaria*, p. 11.

[2] Gunning, *Reminiscences of Cambridge*, I, p. 279.

[3] Parr's *Works*, VIII, p. 150.

friendly terms with well-known reformers such as Horne Tooke and Holcroft,[1] both of whom were put on trial, though not convicted, in 1794. Porson kept out of trouble, but at times he alarmed his friends by expressing violent sentiments, and he had been known to toast Jack Cade in a tavern.

His democratic sentiments found expression in a pamphlet which he published in 1792, entitled *A New Catechism for the Use of the Swinish Multitude, Necessary to be had in all Sties*, or, as he preferred to call it in manuscript copies, *A New Catechism for the Natives of Hampshire*.[2] The reference is to Burke's offensive phrase in his *Reflections* on the French Revolution, about learning being 'trodden down under the hoofs of the swinish multitude', a phrase that his opponents seized upon and did not soon forget. What is your name? The catechism begins.

Answer: Hog or Swine.

Q. Did God make you a Hog?

A. No. God made me in his own image; the Right Honourable Sublime Beautiful made me a Swine.

The Hog or Swine, in reply to further questions, depicts his abject condition under the Hog Drivers and their agents. The allegory is obvious enough, and so are the Jacobinical sentiments, to use the language of the day, of its author.

Porson was closely bound to the opposition by his

[1] In conversation with Holcroft, Porson once maintained that women are by nature inferior to men, and that whipping is beneficial to youth. *Life of Holcroft* (ed. Colby), II, p. 124.

[2] There is a copy in Porson's hand in Trinity Library, and another (which once belonged to Samuel Rogers) in the British Museum (Add. MSS. 30,937).

friendship with Perry as well as by his sympathies. James Perry, an able Aberdonian, had in 1789 acquired *The Morning Chronicle*, a daily paper which he was conducting with ability and success as an organ of the Whig Opposition. When Porson's friendship with him began we do not know, but Perry was among those who subscribed to his annuity in 1792, and not long after Porson was writing for him in *The Morning Chronicle*.

The extent of his contributions to this paper cannot now be discovered, but some of his contemporaries clearly regarded it as considerable. Mathias, 'the Pursuer of Literature', as Porson called him, refers to his 'giving up to Perry what he owed to the world',[1] and Beloe, a friend of Porson's, with some knowledge of the world of journalism, said that 'the world did not know half of what Porson put in print'. Macaulay, half a century after Porson's death, is a less valuable authority. Writing on Pitt, he lays it to his charge that, 'While he was in power the greatest philologist of his age, his own contemporary at Cambridge, was reduced to earn a livelihood by the lowest literary drudgery, and to spend in writing squibs for *The Morning Chronicle* years to which we might have owed an all but perfect text of the whole tragic and comic drama of Athens.'[2] Whether the implications of this sentence are justified or not, cannot now be easily discovered. We would willingly know more about Porson's journalistic activities, how much he wrote, and whether it was in truth to earn a livelihood that he assisted Perry. We may be fairly sure that he was no unwilling drudge in *The Morning Chronicle* office; a liking for Perry, a dislike of Pitt

[1] *Pursuits of Literature*, Dialogue IV, l. 509. Cf. the note on l. 516. [2] Macaulay, *Works* (1866), VII, p. 383.

[43]

and the Tories, a facility for satirical verse and an addiction to late hours made the world of journalism, we may suppose, not uncongenial to him.

On the day of the important debate in the House of Commons which finally determined that the country should go to war with France, Pitt and Dundas, so it was said, came drunk into the House. On this congenial subject Porson produced no fewer than a hundred and one epigrams, which were published in groups at short intervals in *The Morning Chronicle*.[1] The story that they were written in a single night rests on rather flimsy authority, and is disproved by the fact that some of the later epigrams refer to the General Fast proclaimed a week or two after the intoxication of Pitt and Dundas, and later than the publication of the earlier series of epigrams. It is not to be expected that the epigrams should all reach a high level of wit, and in spite of much ingenuity in punning, the joke wears rather thin.

The Morning Chronicle also published three Imitations of Horace, which are held to be certainly from Porson's hand.[2] Imitations of Horace were common enough in the eighteenth century; one might almost say that every educated gentleman tried his hand at them. Porson's are interesting because of their author and the circumstances of their origin. The first is of 'Natis in usum laetitiae scyphis' (C. I, 27). The ode, though preceded by some characteristic witticisms at the expense of

[1] *The Morning Chronicle*, Feb. 20, 1793 (Epigrams 1–11), Feb. 26 (the same repeated), Feb. 28 (12–26), March 2 (27–42), March 4 (43–60), March 7 (61–80), March 13 (81–101). The whole series is in *Spirit of the Public Journals*, 1797, p. 1.

[2] June 25, Aug. 12, Sept. 13, 1794, *Spirit of the Public Journals*, 1797, pp. 107, 147.

Porson's contemporaries, is purely convivial, not topical. Porson offers it as a specimen of a proposed translation of the *Odes*. 'If this sample takes, I mean to publish a translation of the whole by subscription; it will be printed on wire-wove paper, and hot-pressed, not to exceed two volumes quarto. A great number of engravings will be added by the most eminent artists. The obscenities will be left out of the common copies, but printed separately for the use of the curious and critical readers. The passages that have an improper political tendency will be carefully omitted.'

The second imitation is of 'O navis, referent in mare te novi fluctus' (I, 14). The poem was of obvious political reference, though doubtful tendency. Porson's bias can be seen by his reference, not in the original, to the pilot—

> A cub that knows not stem from stern,
> Too high t'obey, too proud to learn.

The third is of the 34th ode of the first book, 'Parcus deorum cultor et infrequens'. How Porson interprets it may be seen from an extract from the introduction, and its contemporary reference is clear enough when we remember the widespread alarm in England at the beginning of the war with France about the supposed spread of republicanism. 'Augustus in the midst of peace and tranquillity felt or feigned an alarm on account of some books written by persons suspected of an attachment to the party of Cato and Brutus, and recommending republican principles. Now Horace having been a colonel in Brutus's army, and being rather too free in professing his religious sentiments, naturally passed for an atheist and a republican. Augustus published an edict to tell his subjects how happy they all were, in spite of the suggestions of malcontents; commanding them to stick close to their old religions; and threatening that whoever was not active in assisting the government, should be treated as an enemy to Church and State. Upon this occasion Horace read—or affected to read, for I will not take my oath to his sincerity—a recantation.'

Among the *Morning Chronicle* pieces attributed to Porson, one of the most amusing is the *Hymn of a New-Made Peer to his Creator*, a somewhat irreverent parody, suited to the period of Pitt's lavish additions to the peerage.[1] The piece is introduced by a quotation from Athenaeus, a fact which supports the attribution to Porson. The uncertain criterion of style has assigned other pieces to his hand.[2] One contribution, a short piece of verse entitled *Burgessiana*, is undoubtedly his, as a copy of it survives in his handwriting. It satirises the Tory politician and journalist James Bland Burgess, who appears to have been a favourite butt of *The Morning Chronicle*. There are other *Burgessiana* which may also be from Porson's hand, but the object of these attacks is now forgotten, and they amuse no longer.

The most curious of these ephemeral productions has still to be mentioned. This is the series of three letters signed 'Mythologus', and entitled *Orgies of Bacchus*, which contemporaries state to be undoubtedly by Porson. The title requires some explanation.

[1] *The Morning Chronicle*, Feb. 23, 1795, *Spirit of the Public Journals*, 1797, p. 250.

[2] Watson assigned to Porson The Miseries of Kingship (Feb. 9, 1793, *Spirit of the Public Journals*, 1797, p. 403) and The Duties of Gentlemen-Soldiers (Aug. 27, 1795). A macaronic dialogue with Echo on the war with France (Sept. 26, 1794) was thought by Beloe to be probably by Porson.

[46]

In the earlier part of 1793 the whole of Cambridge was excited by the trial of William Frend for an alleged attack on the established church. Frend was a Fellow of Jesus, a college then noted as a home of unorthodoxy, the college of Tyrwhitt the Unitarian, and of Gilbert Wakefield the classical scholar, whose political rashness landed him in Dorchester Gaol. Frend in 1793 published a pamphlet entitled *Peace and Union recommended to the Associated Bodies of Republicans and Anti-Republicans*, which contained some very harmless proposals for political reform together with some rather obvious anti-clericalism. It was a time at which most citizens were anxious to show themselves loyal to Church and State. 'Talk of religion,' wrote Porson, 'it is odds you have infidel, blasphemer, atheist, or schismatic, thundered in your ears; touch upon your politics, you will be in luck if you are only charged with a tendency to treason.'[1] It was as easy to be suspected of unorthodoxy in religion as in politics, and one suspicion commonly involved the other. Frend was generally, though without ground, believed to be a republican, and was even suspected of being in treasonable correspondence with the National Convention in France. It was partly political reasons that caused his trial and expulsion from the University.

He was summoned before the Vice-Chancellor's Court by the evangelical and autocratic Isaac Milner, President of Queens'; among the assessors was Dr Postlethwaite, and the promoter, or prosecutor, was Dr Kipling, who acted as deputy to the absentee Regius professor of Divinity, Bishop Watson. Dr Kipling, whose incompetence and bad latinity were alike notorious, was the subject of general dislike and mockery in Cambridge.

[1] *Orgies of Bacchus, Spirit of the Public Journals*, 1797, p. 266.

On this occasion, though Frend was condemned and expelled from the University, Dr Kipling conducted the prosecution so badly that it was generally agreed that the trial was no credit to orthodoxy or to the University. It was not only Coleridge and the other undergraduates in the Senate House gallery who sympathised with Frend.

An interest in the trial was not confined to Cambridge. *The Morning Chronicle* reported it, and printed some attacks on Dr Kipling, probably from Porson's hand. A few years before, Kipling had published, at great expense to the University, a facsimile of Beza's manuscript of the New Testament,[1] in the Preface to which he had committed some mistakes in Latin which were not easily forgotten by Cambridge and were brought up by Frend at the trial. As a result of an unfortunate dative or ablative form the deputy professor won the nickname of Dr Paginibus, and Porson (if he was the author) sent to *The Morning Chronicle* an epigram in the manner of the *Epistolae Obscurorum Virorum*, in which the words italicised are mistakes actually made by Kipling:

> *Paginibus* nostris dicitis mihi menda quod insunt:
> At non in recto vos puto esse, viri.
> Nam primum: iurat, cetera *ut* testimonia *omitto*
> Milnerus quod sum doctus ego et sapiens.
> Classicus haud es, aiunt. Quid si non sum? in sacrosancta
> Non *ullo* tergum verto theologia.[2]

A month later[3] appeared a mock defence of Kipling, in the form of a Latin letter from Magister Ortvinus

[1] For Porson's opinion of this production see his letter to *The Gentleman's Magazine*, Oct. 1788 (*Correspondence*, p. 23).

[2] *The Morning Chronicle*, June 19, 1793.   [3] July 18.

Gratius, the recipient of the letters of the Obscure Men. This, and the *Ode to Dr Kipling*, in the style of the Laureate (Pye),[1] may well be by Porson.

One of the sentences in Frend's pamphlet which gave colour to the charge of the prosecution was that which ran thus: 'The same passions will everywhere produce on certain minds the same effect: and the priest, in every age, whether he celebrates the orgies of Bacchus or solemnises the Eucharist, will, should either his victims, or his allowance fail, oppose in either case every truth which threatens to undermine his altars or weaken his sacerdotal authority.' This sentence gave Porson the subject of the three letters, which appeared in 1793 and 1794.[2] 'As I apprehend', he wrote, 'that many of your readers may be in as great doubt as I was, concerning these same Orgies of Bacchus, I hope the following brief sketch will not displease them.' Apart from some incidental jibes at poor Kipling, the letters do not treat directly the topical issue; they consist of a learned though flippant account of the career of the god Bacchus, and the spread of his worship, written in terms that are clearly meant to suggest Christianity and its founder.

It is not surprising that Porson's clerical biographers have been shocked by the *Orgies*, that Kidd was forced to assume that Porson's brain was overclouded when he wrote them, that Luard advised that they be left unread, and that Watson printed an objectionable portion in a Latin translation. It would be easy to mock at the susceptibilities of these admirers, but it is not easy to

---

[1] *The Morning Chronicle*, June 10 and 28, 1793.

[2] Nov. 21, 1793, Dec. 27, 1793 and Sept. 27, 1794, *Spirit of the Public Journals*, 1797, pp. 261f.

say what Porson's religious views were, for he was always reticent on this subject. In his boyhood, we are told, he had written 'hymns and grave reflections... tracing out the adorable nature of the First Cause',[1] but this early piety seems to have faded away. His admiring friend Kidd is anxious to defend him against the charge of infidelity, and refers to three passages in the *Letters to Travis* as proving his Christian sentiments. But, as reference to the context shows, they do not give much support to his contention, and one of them has a distinctly Gibbonian flavour: 'The merits of the martyr' (he is writing of Cyprian) 'threw a shade over the defects of the author, and the veneration that ought to have been confined to his piety was extended to his writings.'[2]

An obituarist even goes so far as to say that Porson was 'truly and actively pious', and tells us that 'in no moment the most unguarded was he ever known to utter a single expression of discontent at the Establishment, of derision of those who thought differently from himself, much less of profanation or impiety'. This may perhaps be true of his conversation, but the *Orgies of Bacchus* give a different impression. We may mention too a passage in the *Catechism for the Swinish Multitude*, which Watson omits, though he quotes the rest of the pamphlet. '*Q.* Do they themselves' [the 'Ministers of Peace', the clergy that is] 'believe what they teach you? (Hog shakes his head). Why do you hesitate? Do they themselves believe what they teach you?—They believe

---

[1] Kidd, *Imperfect Outline*, p. x.
[2] *Letters to Travis*, p. 266. Cf. Gibbon, ch. XXIII: 'The merit of a seasonable conversion was allowed to supply the defects of a candidate.'

that it is for their own interest that we should believe it.'
In fact we may say of Porson what he himself said of his
favourite Euripides, who was suspected of impiety in
his day: 'Sive hoc crimen verum, sive falsum esset,
negari non potest, eum suspicioni nimium loci dedisse.'[1]

Luard believed that the *Orgies* were written 'in a sort
of wanton spirit of opposition which possessed him at
the time', and do not represent his real opinions. This
explanation need not at once be set aside as a clergyman's
attempt to explain away what he disapproves of. The
situation at the end of the century was somewhat
peculiar, and divided right and left wings both in religion
and politics more sharply than is usual in this country.
When the patriotism of Tories and the orthodoxy of
Churchmen were unusually fervent, liberal-minded men
might be driven into an equally fervent opposition and
express themselves more strongly than they would at
other times. Moreover, Porson had suffered himself
from Dr Postlethwaite, who had a part in the trial of
Frend, and no doubt was a representative of the rather
timid orthodoxy then prevalent at Cambridge. But the
spirit of opposition which Porson manifested in 1793,
though more violent than at other times, cannot be
said to be out of keeping with the rest of his life.

Porson was certainly something of an anti-clerical.
As for his theological views, it may be assumed they
were not orthodox, but further than that we cannot go.
Eighteenth-century Cambridge had seen a succession
of unorthodox theologians from Whiston to Tyrwhitt.
Whether they went under the name of Arians, Socinians
or Unitarians, their main objection was to the doctrine
of the Trinity. And it may well be that Porson's refusal

[1] *Adversaria*, p. 26.

to take orders and his distaste for subscription rested on a dislike for this article of faith.[1] On the other hand, he is said to have once remarked that if the New Testament was to settle the matter and words had any meaning, the Socinians were wrong; and he never severed his connection with the Church of England, as did some of his contemporaries, Frend for one. He attended chapel at Trinity towards the end of his life, and 'repeated the responses aloud in a grave and sonorous manner, and so as to be heard all over the chapel'.[2] And it is known that once, when staying with his sister, he received the Sacrament.

Porson did not present a clear and unequivocal attitude on religion, nor was he ever willing to express an opinion on it. He may perhaps rightly be considered a conscientious agnostic on theological matters. Protagoras professed himself unable to decide whether the gods existed or not; there were many things that prevented one from knowing, the obscurity of the subject and the shortness of human life. So too Porson once remarked: 'I found that I should require about fifty years' reading to make myself thoroughly acquainted with divinity, to satisfy my mind on all points, and therefore I gave it up. There are fellows who go into the pulpit assuming everything and knowing nothing; but I would not do so.'[3]

[1] There is a story that Porson and a friend were discussing the mystery of the Trinity when a buggy passed containing three men. 'There', said the friend, 'is an illustration of the Trinity.' 'No,' said Porson, 'it ought to be one man in three buggies.' But Porson has not an exclusive claim to this saying.

[2] Pryme, *Autobiographic Recollections*, p. 86.

[3] Maltby, *Porsoniana*, p. 305.

VI

In 1796 Porson surprised his friends by marrying. His bride was the sister of his friend Perry; she had married a bookbinder called Lunan, but had divorced him by Scots law, and was now living with her brother in Lancaster Court. Porson's marriage to her was to have been kept a secret; but we are curiously well informed about his doings on the day of the wedding. The abundance of information is indeed embarrassing, for the accounts conflict with one another. The fullest story is that of Pryse Gordon, who had it from his brother George, a friend of Porson's.

On the day before the wedding, according to his story, Porson was sitting smoking in his favourite haunt, the Cider Cellar in Maiden Lane, when he suddenly said to Gordon: 'Friend George, do you not think the widow Lunan an agreeable sort of personage as times go?' Gordon said something favourable about the lady, and Porson proceeded: 'In that case, you must meet me to-morrow morning at St Martin's in the Fields at eight o'clock.' The next morning Gordon appeared at the church and found Porson with Mrs Lunan and a female friend, and the clergyman ready to perform the ceremony. After it was over the bride and her friend went out by one door, and Porson with Gordon by another. Porson had meant to keep the wedding secret for fear of offending Perry, but Gordon insisted that he should know of it, and eventually Porson consented to go with him to Lancaster Court and settle things with his brother-in-law. Perry, though a little hurt, was soon pacified, and provided dinner for the newly married couple.

This is Gordon's account.[1] It is certainly wrong in one detail. Porson was married not in St Martin-in-the-Fields, but in St Clement Danes. The marriage was by licence, and took place on November 24, 1796.[2] The latter part of the story also is contradicted by other evidence, in this case no more reliable than that of Gordon. According to Beloe, 'it is a well-known fact that he spent the day of his marriage with a very learned friend, now a judge'.[3] And yet another account says that he dined with Raine, Master of the Charterhouse, and after dining pulled out his watch and said: 'God bless me, I was married to-day and was engaged to dine with my wife.'[4]

The accounts cannot be reconciled, and the discrepancy reminds us of the unreliability of the anecdotists and memoir-writers to whom we owe so much of our knowledge of Porson. Two further stories of his wedding-day can be reconciled with the other accounts, though we may reserve judgment as to their accuracy. Maltby saw Porson one forenoon in Covent Garden dressed in a pea-green coat; it was the day of his wedding, as Maltby afterwards learnt, though Porson said nothing about it. Porson had just bought off a stall a copy of the Rabelaisian satire *Le Moyen de Parvenir*; holding it up he called to Maltby: 'These are the sort of

---

[1] Gordon, *Personal Memoirs*, I, p. 280.
[2] In the register Mrs Lunan is described as Mary Pirie, single woman. Perry's father in Aberdeen spelt his name Pirie.
[3] *The Sexagenarian*, I, p. 230.
[4] Barker's MS. *Porsoniana*.

books to buy.' Finally it is said that at the end of the day he went to the Cider Cellar and sat there drinking until eight o'clock the next morning. Since this last story is not wholly creditable to Porson, it should be said that it rests on very poor evidence. It was not heard of till over forty years after Porson's marriage, in 1837, when E. H. Barker, in the debtors' prison, heard it from a Mr Moore, a fellow prisoner. When we remember that Porson's wedding was kept secret for a time, and its date was not known, we cannot help being sceptical about Mr Moore's story.

However he spent the first evening of his wedded life, Porson is said to have made a good husband. He lived at Lancaster Court with his wife and brother-in-law, and became more regular in his habits under the influence of matrimony. But his married life was very short, for his wife died in April 1797, and the brief episode had little influence on him. He relapsed into those irregular and convivial habits for which he was notorious.

That Porson drank freely and indiscriminately has never been denied. Horne Tooke said that he would drink ink rather than nothing at all, and Pryse Gordon that the quality of the drink was immaterial so long as he had quantity. But his lack of discrimination has perhaps been exaggerated; we need not believe it when we read that he drank embrocation and eye-water and 'Velno's Vegetable Spirits'. Even the well-known story of his drinking methylated spirits appears somewhat doubtful on inspection. Porson, finding a bottle in the bedroom of his host's wife, drank it up and pronounced it the best gin he had ever tasted; it was the wife who next day told her husband that it was 'spirits of wine for the lamp'.

Porson's tastes were probably not so exotic, and may be expressed in his own couplet:

> When ale and wine are gone and spent
> Small beer is then most excellent.

His drinking was probably begun as a solace for sleeplessness; and though it often exceeded the bounds of propriety, it would not be correct to call Porson a habitual drunkard. He could abstain if he wished, and he did not drink to excess when by himself. But he was not always welcome in society; with his red nose and his shabby appearance he looked the typical debauchee and was sometimes refused admittance to his friends' houses. He was at times to be seen with a patch of brown paper on his nose, and there is a letter extant in which he refers facetiously to the state of his face, and refuses the invitation of a friend on the grounds that 'I have put myself under a regimen of abstinence till my poor nose recovers its quondam colour and compass'.[1]

When he did come to a friend's house it was not easy to get rid of him. It was no use inviting him, as Horne Tooke once did, after he had stayed up the previous three nights, for he was perfectly willing to sit through a fourth. On one occasion, when he had visited a friend by mistake a day too early, he sat up all night drinking, smoking and reading, and was ready for the party the next day.

In company Porson was sometimes dull and boorish, but when his companions were congenial and he had drunk well he could be brilliant and entertaining. He was a good talker when in the mood for it, but no faithful admirer has preserved his table talk, and only a few sorry scraps torn from their context have survived in

[1] *Correspondence*, p. 116.

the recollections of Samuel Rogers. On the whole, Porson's conversation was not deep or weighty: he was not a Johnson or a Coleridge, edifying his listeners with judgments on life and literature. He preferred to amuse them with epigrams and witticisms, and to produce from the stores of his memory long passages of poetry and prose. He could recite line after line of Greek, Latin, French and English, and knew the lighter literature of his day as well as he knew Shakespeare and the Greek tragedians. He could repeat, so it is said, the whole of *Roderick Random*, as well as other more ephemeral productions of the day. Unfortunately, he was inclined to forget his audience, and to continue his recitations when they were no longer desired.

Porson's company was not an unmixed blessing. His host had to be prepared for rudeness as well as late hours and recitations. A friend in Cambridge who had entertained him was told, as the professor left: 'Sir, you have sat up all night, and have the pleasure of knowing that you have not said a single word worth hearing during the whole of it.'[1] In argument, Porson was a formidable opponent with a gift for effective repartee. 'Mr Porson,' said someone, after a heated argument, 'my opinion of you is contemptible.' 'I know no opinion of yours that is not contemptible', answered Porson. Even his silence could be alarming, as the painter Kirkby once found. Porson had been silent for a time, and Kirkby foolishly said: 'Come, professor, say a good thing.' Porson answered nothing, but fixed his eyes on Kirkby, until the latter was forced in shame to leave the room.

But in spite of the disadvantages of his company,

[1] See *Etoniana* 33, p. 516.

Porson was a welcome guest at the houses of scholars and literary men. More surprisingly, he was a favourite with their wives and sisters. He would amuse them with conundrums and charades, and sometimes present them with these compositions written out in his small and neat hand. In London, his favourite haunt was the Cider Cellar in Maiden Lane where, according to the story, he spent the night of his wedding-day. With its portrait of Porson, and its Latin motto over the doorway which he had suggested, it was particularly associated with him, and preserved his memory after his death, until the building was absorbed in the extension of the Adelphi Theatre. Another favourite resort was the Bristol coffee-house in Cockspur Street, where a club called the 'Anonymous', consisting of Porson and a few intimate friends, used to meet. It was a convivial but learned club, given to accompanying toasts with quotations from Shakespeare. Thus, when Porson had published his *Hecuba*, and Wakefield was known to be preparing an attack on it, the club was given the toast of 'my friend Gilbert Wakefield, "What's Hecuba to him or he to Hecuba?"'

Porson's friends were, except for the Scotsmen Perry and Gordon, mostly scholarly clerics, such as Burney, Raine and Cleaver Banks. He did not move in smart society, and refused to go to Holland House to meet Charles James Fox; allied though the two were in political views and scholarly interests, they never became acquainted. It was left to a less retiring scholar, Gilbert Wakefield, to become Fox's correspondent and adviser on classical literature. Porson was however acquainted with Fox's nephew Lord Holland, for he was one of the original members of a club called The King of Clubs, founded in 1798, at which Holland and other intellectual Whigs of the day met for dinner and conversation.[1] Once Porson went to an evening party in the West End, where he entertained some fashionable ladies by reciting old popular songs, drank a great deal, and after leaving the party, was sick in Piccadilly. Once he was even seen, shabby and ill at ease, in the assembly room at Bath.

Normally he did not go far afield, and grew more and more disinclined to travel. In 1799 there was a rumour current that he had been asked to go to Constantinople to examine the Greek manuscripts there, but this was apparently a false story put into circulation by Bishop Tomline, Pitt's tutor and biographer, a man whom Porson regarded with detestation.[2] If he had been asked, he would not willingly have accepted, for he could not be persuaded even to go to Paris, though he wanted to consult some manuscripts there. Sometimes he would stay with Burney at Greenwich, or at Merton in his brother-in-law's country house. It was here that the fire occurred which destroyed some of his papers, including his transcript of Photius, on which he had spent many years. The Codex Galeanus itself, which he had borrowed from Trinity Library, he had with him; the transcript, only just completed, was left at Perry's. Porson straightway set his hand to repairing the loss by producing another copy, which still survives, a monument of patience and accuracy, in the library of Trinity.

[1] Lady Seymour, *The Pope of Holland House*, p. 333.

[2] See *Life of Wilberforce*, II, p. 344, and Maltby, *Porsoniana*, p. 319. Tomline had changed his name from Pretyman on receipt of a legacy from a man who, it was said, had only seen him once. Porson remarked that if he had seen him twice he would not have left the legacy.

In later life Porson paid one or two visits to his married sister in Norfolk; when staying with her he would drink moderately, go to church, and make himself useful in the garden. To his sister he displayed a side of his character often hidden. The following letter, with its domestic trivialities, has a touch of geniality not often found in Porson's writing.

Dear Sister,

I arrived safely in London the morning after I left Coltishall, and have had no complaint of any consequence since my arrival, except a violent cold, which, however, is now going off. I have not yet exhausted all my butter, but as it is rather hard I am obliged to toast my bread. If you have a mind to send me a turkey, pray send one that may do our dear county some credit. Direct to me, No. 5, Essex Court, Temple, or in his absence, to be left at Mr Temple's, hairdresser. I find very little linen of mine that wants repairing, but I will shortly look about me and send you some fresh cloth, the great coat and all. You and your people will, I suppose, be very busy in keeping Christmas at the time you receive this. Give them all my duty respectfully and respectively, and tell Mr Woodcock that of late I have been drinking London porter, which is pretty drink enough, but not to be named of a day with the Norfolk brewage.

Non etenim ignoro quid distent aera lupinis.

Siday will explain this scrap of Horace to you. My compliments to Dr Grape and Mr Blake. I am, dear Sister,

Your affectionate brother
R. PORSON.

24 Dec. 1804.

P.S. Write me a line at your leisure to inform me of our father's health, and whether you received the inclosed safe.[1]

[1] *Correspondence*, p. 103. Corrected from original in Trinity College Library.

Porson's brothers seem to have been less sympathetic to him, and we do not hear of his ever going to see them. His younger brother Thomas had been in his turn educated first by Summers then by Hewitt, and had a short career as schoolmaster before his early death. In 1788 Mrs Hewitt wrote to Porson, asking if he could help in getting a position for his brother as assistant in a school; Porson replied at some length, though doubtful if he could do much to help.[1] He sought the aid of Dr Parr, who had more influence in the scholastic world, but whether it was due to Parr or to Porson or to neither that Thomas obtained his first post at Wymondham, we do not know. The older brother Henry complained that though he wrote to Dick, Dick never wrote to him. However, when Henry Porson died at an early age leaving some orphaned children, Richard dutifully assisted them.

His unreadiness to write letters was noted not by his family only. Foreign scholars sent him elaborate and courteous letters, sometimes enclosing their own books, and received no reply or acknowledgment. Hermann, Heyne, Eichstädt and Tittmann wrote from Germany, Gail and Villoison from France. Only the last, so far as we know, was answered. Porson could be polite and generous to foreigners when he wished, and Villoison was delighted to receive a copy of the Grenville *Homer*, and of Porson's *Medea*. We also find Wyttenbach writing to Cleaver Banks to thank him for copies of Porson's books, sent by Banks, and mentioning his intention of sending to Porson a copy of his own *Life of Ruhnken*—the scholar who in his old age had helped the young Porson.[2]

---

[1] See p. 113. [2] *Wyttenbachii Epistolae*, I, p. 16.

Porson was proud and sensitive, and regarded flattery with distaste. A sure way of annoying him was to praise him, and complimentary letters from strangers he ignored. He was perhaps inclined to be suspicious of those he did not know, but to his friends he showed no lack of generosity, and was always willing to impart information and give assistance. Though his writing has the appearance of ease, he seems to have composed only with difficulty, and to have been unable often to summon up the necessary energy. His letters were generally short, clear and businesslike, though in writing to scholars he adopts a more literary style. As an example of his more ornamental manner, we may quote the graceful letter of congratulation to Martin Davy, M.D., written on his election to the mastership of Caius.

Dear Doctor,

I heartily congratulate you, and your friends, and the College, and the University, on your well deserved promotion, Ζηλῶ τε σοῦ μὲν 'Ελλάδ', 'Ελλάδος δὲ σέ. I shall not trespass upon your time with a long letter, occupied as I take it for granted you must be with the circumstances attendant on your elevation, and with the swarm of addresses that invade you from all quarters. Neither shall I amuse myself with foretelling the future glories of your reign. I never but once ventured on a similar prediction, and then my success was such as completely discouraged me from setting up for a prophet again. But a passage from Cicero had long lain rusting in my mind, which passage I had almost despaired of introducing, when lo! the occasion, which the gods hardly durst have promised to my wishes, revolving time threw in my way. Est tibi gravis adversaria constituta et parata, incredibilis quaedam expectatio: quam tu una re facillime vinces, si hoc statueris, quarum laudum gloriam adamaris, quibus artibus

eae laudes comparantur, in iis esse laborandum.   *   *
*   *   *   *   *   *   *   *   *   *   *
*   *   *   *   *   *   is gone to Brighton for
the benefit of his health, which had been for some time in
a very precarious state; but I learn that he has found, what he
could not, it seems, find in London, a physician, whose
prescriptions have done him some good. And now we are
talking of physicians, I have been lately studying anatomy.
The last subject I cut up was human nature; and I discovered,
that all the wars, and murders, and bloodshed, and quarrels,
and cruelties, that are incident to sickly mortals (mortalibus
aegris) arise from their follies, vices and crimes; and if the
doctors would undertake to purge and correct the humours
which feed those follies, pamper those vices, and engender
those crimes, the fee must be large indeed, that I should
grudge them;

>   Εἰ δ' Ἀσκληπιάδαις τοῦτό γ' ἔδωκε θεὸς
>   Ἰᾶσθαι κακότητα καὶ ἀτηρὰς φρένας ἀνδρῶν,
>   Πολλοὺς ἂν μισθοὺς καὶ μεγάλους ἔφερον.

But I am committing the very fault I promised to avoid.
I wish you long life and health to wear your new dignity to
the mutual satisfaction of yourself and the public, and I
remain,
                    Dear Doctor,
               Your faithful friend, and humble servant,
                              R. PORSON.[1]

[1] *Correspondence*, p. 83, from Kidd, *Tracts and Criticisms*, p. 330.
Kidd quotes it with the omission in the middle. The original
does not survive.

VII

IT would be easy to suppose that Porson's convivial
habits left him little time or inclination for study.
Moreover, he was often in poor health; as early as 1798
we find a contemporary noting in his diary, 'health of
Porson precarious',[1] and he himself writes to a friend
in 1802 that he has 'been at death's door'.[2] We may
wonder not that he produced so little but that he produced anything at all. He did not, however, spend all
his days and nights convivially. Sometimes he shut
himself up in his rooms and worked for days on end,
as when he was collating the Harleian MS. of the
Odyssey for the Grenville *Homer*. At Cambridge, we
are told, when in a reading humour he would sit up all
night for about ten days, and go to bed for a few hours
after morning chapel.[3] But his reading was not regular,
and at times he would give up Greek and read nothing
but light literature.

Maty's Review had ceased to exist, but reviews of
classical books by Porson appeared occasionally in a
more important periodical, *The Monthly Review*. In
1788 he there reviewed Robertson's *Parian Chronicle*,
in 1793 Edwards's edition of Plutarch, *De Educatione
Puerorum*, and in the next year Payne Knight's *Analytical
Essay on the Greek Alphabet*. To the etymological specu-
lations of Payne Knight, otherwise known as landscape

---

[1] *Life of Holcroft* (ed. Colby), II, p. 139.
[2] *Correspondence*, p. 71.
[3] Pryme, *Autobiographic Recollections*, p. 86.

gardener and dilettante, Porson is not unfavourable; he pays him the compliment of a long review and concludes by saying that his errors are sometimes more to the point than the successful inquiries of others. This review and that of Robertson's book attest Porson's interest in inscriptions; though the latter does not display his epigraphical learning so much as his dialectical skill in exposing the unsound arguments of Mr Robertson.[1]

There were other anonymous reviews in which Porson is said to have had a hand, and some contributions by Burney to *The Monthly Review*, superior in scholarship to his ordinary work, were thought to owe their distinction to Porson's help. But until 1790 Porson had done little to make known his peculiar gifts in classical criticism beyond the learned circles of Cambridge and London. He won a wider fame by the publication of his Appendix to Toup's *Suidas*. He had read with interest and admiration the *Emendations of Suidas* by Jonathan Toup, and when in 1790 a new edition was published, it was with an appendix containing Porson's notes, which he had written and sent to the Oxford Press three years before, in 1787, under the impression that an edition was then in preparation.

His early project of editing Aeschylus had never been wholly abandoned, and there was a general expectation that he would produce a complete edition, with notes, scholia, and fragments. But the public was doomed to disappointment. As early as 1792 he made an agreement

---

[1] The review of *The Sovereign*, by C. S. Pybus, in *The Monthly Review*, December 1800, is wrongly ascribed to Porson by Kidd and others. S. Butler (*The Monthly Review*, January 1818) states that it is not the work of Porson, and in the editor's copy in the Bodleian it is, I am informed, ascribed to another writer.

with the London booksellers for an octavo edition,[1] and
the text in two volumes was actually printed by Foulis
of Glasgow in 1794, but was not published for some
years. In 1795, however, a magnificent folio edition of
Aeschylus appeared from Foulis, 'without the name of
any editor in the title, without a line of preface, without
a single note, without the scholia and without the
fragments'.[2] The text, which improved on Stanley's in
many places, was presumed to be Porson's, and later
was found to agree substantially with the smaller edition.
But the publication was unauthorised, and Porson never
assumed any responsibility for it.[3]

Probably he was not satisfied with his text, and was
too indolent to complete the edition and too conscientious to allow it to be published in an imperfect
state. Hence the long delay. Eventually the booksellers
insisted on the publication of the text in octavo, and it
appeared, without Porson's name, in 1806. 'It was
given to the world', says Kidd, 'with his knowledge,
and with a sort of half-faced consent.'[4] It was still the
bare text, with a Latin translation, but without notes
or fragments; for these the public waited in vain, while
the intended preface, long pondered over, was never
committed to paper.

Meanwhile Porson had projected a complete edition
of Euripides, a poet with whom he had more sympathy

[1] See *Correspondence*, p. 106. In a letter of 1791 (printed
p. 117) Porson refers to some business to be discussed with the
booksellers, probably the edition of Aeschylus.

[2] [Burney] in *The Monthly Review*, February 1796.

[3] There is said to have been a Choephori Glasg. 1777 with
Porson's text. The date is presumed to be a fraud. [Dobree] in
The Monthly Review, June 1807.

[4] *Tracts and Criticisms*, p. lxix.

than he had with Aeschylus. His original intention was to publish each play separately, and to add a dissertation on Greek metres. He began with the *Hecuba*, to which, as we have seen, he devoted special attention in his praelection; his edition appeared in 1797 in unassuming form, without his name, and described as being designed 'in usum studiosae iuventutis'—the reverse affectation to Housman's 'editorum in usum'. There was a preface dealing chiefly with the admissibility of anapaests in the tragic senarius. Previous to Porson there had been two schools of thought on the subject, one allowing anapaests in every foot but the last, the other admitting them to all the odd feet. Porson claimed that, except in the case of proper names, anapaests were admissible only in the first foot, and showed how few and how easily emended were the apparent exceptions.

Among those who read the new edition was Gilbert Wakefield, who was grievously disappointed to find none of his own conjectures mentioned. Porson was no enemy of Wakefield; he was on good terms with him personally, and probably sympathised with his views; it was in fact out of kindness that he had not mentioned him in the *Hecuba*, for he could hardly have mentioned him favourably. But Wakefield was one of those persons born to cause trouble to themselves and to all with whom they come in contact. He rushed into print with a pamphlet entitled *In Euripidis Hecubam Londini nuper publicatam Diatribe Extemporalis*, an apt title, if the pamphlet, as we are told, was written in a few hours.[1] It is a display of vanity and confidence so naïve as to be almost unobjectionable. Porson did not trouble to reply, but in the second edition of the *Hecuba* he answered

[1] Wakefield's *Memoirs* (1804), vol. II, p. 100.

briefly those criticisms that were worth answering; for though Wakefield's own conjectures were without exception bad, he did occasionally point to a weak spot in Porson's edition.

The *Hecuba* aroused a more formidable opponent than Gilbert Wakefield. Gottfried Hermann of Leipzig had published in 1796, at the age of twenty-four, an elaborate treatise on metres, which Elmsley described as 'a book of which too much ill cannot easily be said, and which contains a smaller quantity of useful and solid information in proportion to its bulk, than any elementary treatise, on any subject, which we remember to have seen'. On the appearance of Porson's *Hecuba*, Hermann rapidly produced a rival edition (1800), with a Preface attacking Porson's opinions. Hermann wanted to know not only what the Greeks regarded as admissible but also why they so regarded it. Seeing no reason why they should have rejected anapaests, he admitted them to every foot except the last. Porson had no use for a priori theories, but preferred the more fruitful method of studying what the Greeks actually wrote. Aided by a natural feeling for rhythm and a consciousness of the fallibility of scribes, he achieved a success that vindicated his method of observation as far more valuable than Hermann's ambitious systematising.

Porson was not a little annoyed at Hermann's attack, and later English scholars have blamed the German for his presumption. His *Hecuba* was no more presumptuous than Headlam's attack on Verrall, written at about the same age, but in controversies like this it is more important to be right than to be modest. And though on some of the points in question two opinions are possible, Hermann on the whole has little to show on his side. He lived to learn from Porson and to acknowledge his merits, though he and his pupils retained a certain bias against the English scholars. The nationalist bias was certainly not absent on the other side; Porson did not care for the Germans and their scholarship,[1] and his followers were confident that the Preface to *Hecuba* had said the last word on the iambic senarius.

Porson resented Hermann's attack, and circulated an epigram on him after the model of Phocylides:

Νήϊδες ἐστὲ μέτρων, ὦ Τεύτονες· οὐχ ὃ μὲν, ὃς δ' οὔ·
Πάντες, πλὴν ῞ΕΡΜΑΝΝΟΣ· ὃ δ' ῞ΕΡΜΑΝΝΟΣ σφόδρα Τεύτων.

> The Germans in Greek
> Are sadly to seek;
> Not five in five score,
> But ninety-five more:
> All; save only HERMAN,
> And HERMAN's a German.

'It is a known principle', he proceeds, after quoting these two versions in a letter to Andrew Dalzel of Edinburgh, 'that the iambic may be resolved into a tribrach in any place but the last. As Mr Herman has not given any striking instances in his incomparable treatise, I shall try to supply the defect:

῾Ο μετρικὸς, ὃ σοφὸς ἄτοπα γέγραφε περὶ μέτρων.
῾Ο μετρικὸς ἄμετρος, ὃ σοφὸς ἄσοφος ἐγένετο.[2]

Hermann's *Hecuba* had the effect of producing in 1802 a second edition of Porson's book, with a greatly enlarged Preface supporting those views originally put forward with a spareness which contrasted markedly with Hermann's prolixity. The Supplement to the

---

[1] οὗτοι δ' εἰσὶν συοβοιωτοὶ κρουπεζοφόρων γένος ἀνδρῶν, said Porson of the Germans, quoting Cratinus with his own emendation.
[2] *Correspondence*, p. 87.

Preface takes the place of the projected Dissertation on Metres; it discusses the laws of iambic, trochaic and anapaestic verse in both tragedy and comedy, and includes the formulation of the law for which Porson is perhaps chiefly remembered. In a note on line 347 he had re-marked in the first edition that there were very few lines like the first line of the *Ion*, "Ἄτλας ὁ χαλκέοισι νώτοις οὐρανόν. In the second Preface this observation becomes the canon that we know as Porson's law or the law of the final cretic. It is now familiar to any school-boy who learns to write Greek verse, but that it was by no means obvious even to the best scholars before that day is shown by Porson's undergraduate iambics already referred to, and by the fact that Bentley could quote (presumably from memory) as a line of Euripides, Διόνυσον οὐκ ἔφασκον εἶναι τοῦ Διός.[1]

Meanwhile three other plays had been published, the *Orestes* in 1798, the *Phoenissae* in 1799, and the *Medea* in 1801, the last play being the first to be printed at the Cambridge Press. Here the series ended. After the second edition of the *Hecuba* Porson published nothing.[2] For reasons which need not be repeated Porson in his later years was scarcely capable of the effort necessary for literary production, and he appears to have abandoned altogether the idea of completing his Euripides.

He was known to be a lover of Aristophanes, and towards the end of his life was thought to be preparing an edition of the comedies, for which, so it was said, he had been offered £3000 by the London booksellers.

---

[1] *Epistola ad Millium*. Bentley's *Works* (ed. Dyce), II, p. 261. The line should end ἐκφῦναι Διός (*Bacch.* 27).

[2] In October 1802 he sent to *The Monthly Magazine* a letter signed John Nic. Dawes, correcting a mistake in his *Medea*.

In 1805 his scholarly friends were inquiring, How goes the Aristophanes? But their inquiries were in vain, for though he had a good deal of material collected in his notebooks and more in his head, Porson never troubled to put it together.

It remains to record some minor literary productions. It has already been mentioned that Porson saw through the press an English edition of Heyne's *Virgil* (1793). This was largely mechanical labour, and did not add to his reputation, for the work was ill done, and there were many misprints to be found in the published volumes. Whether this was the fault of the corrector, or, as Porson himself maintained, of the printer, we cannot say. At the time when he was engaged on Euripides he was asked to undertake the collation of the Harleian manuscript of the *Odyssey* (Codex Harleianus 5674), to be appended to the magnificent Oxford edition known as the Grenville *Homer*, which appeared in 1801. In return for the accomplishment of this task, he received a large paper copy of the Homer and the sum of fifty guineas.[1]

How long he continued to contribute to *The Morning Chronicle* we cannot say. One characteristic contribution dates from 1796. It was the time of Ireland's Shakespeare forgeries. William Ireland had published some documents, including a new play, which he claimed were from the hand of Shakespeare and had been found by Ireland's son Samuel in an old chest. Eminent scholars and literary men were deceived, including Dr Parr and Boswell, the latter of whom knelt down with a glass of brandy in one hand and kissed the documents in venera-

[1] Simpson, *Proof reading in the sixteenth, seventeenth and eighteenth centuries*, p. 217.

tion. Porson, when asked to subscribe his name to a declaration that the documents were genuine, refused on the ground that he detested subscriptions of all kinds, especially subscriptions to Articles of Faith. He sent to *The Morning Chronicle* a letter purporting to come from one S. England, who claimed that a friend of his had discovered in an old trunk some lost plays of Sophocles, and enclosed a specimen consisting of twelve iambic lines. This was in fact Porson's Greek version of the nursery poem Three Children Sliding on the Ice. The lines were accompanied with a Latin translation, a parody of the literal versions to be found in editions of Greek tragedy of that day.

Porson was known to his contemporaries as a wit and a versifier, and several satirical pieces by him were in circulation. We may quote the pleasant verse dialogue in which he ridiculed the mutual admiration of Anna Seward, the 'Swan of Lichfield', and the poet Hayley:

> Miss Seward loquitur:
>
> Tuneful poet, Britain's glory,
> Mr Hayley, that is you.
>
> Hayley respondet:
>
> Ma'am you carry all before ye,
> Trust me, Lichfield swan, you do.
>
> Miss Seward:
>
> Ode, didactic, epic, sonnet,
> Mr Hayley, you're divine.
>
> Hayley:
>
> Ma'am, I'll take my oath upon it,
> You yourself are all the Nine.[1]

[1] Printed in Beloe, *The Sexagenarian*, II, p. 310. I have emended 'before you' to 'before ye'.

It was natural enough that Porson's name should become attached to many of the anonymous verses and jeux d'esprit then current. He was for instance widely believed to be the author of *Eloisa en Dishabille*, 'A profligate parody', to quote the original advertisement, 'of Mr Pope's Epistle from Eloisa to Abelard.'[1] This is a paraphrase in smooth anapaestic doggerel; its impropriety offends by its quality rather than its quantity. Porson himself denied the authorship more than once in conversation, and once, we are told, attributed it to George Tierney the Whig politician.[2] Moreover, he left a manuscript note on the subject. He had found it stated in print that the Greek professor at Cambridge had written a parody on Pope's *Eloisa*; he pointed out that the verses were printed in 1780, when he was still an undergraduate, and went on: 'If the author should say that he only meant that the person who wrote the parody is now Greek professor, I shall pass over the clumsiness of the expression, and only desire him to produce his proofs of the latter fact. This I know that I have several times heard Mr Porson seriously disown all share whatever in the composition of that parody and all knowledge of its author.' Porson's biographer justly remarks that he might have denied the authorship with less circumlocution, and suspects that Porson was anxious to disown a production of his youth which did him little credit. The truth about the authorship was not known then and can be known even less to-day. Yet even if we acquit

[1] It was first printed in 1780. The British Museum copy is dated 1822.

[2] Genest, *Some Account of the English Stage*, VI, p. 442. It was attributed to Mr Coffin of Exeter by the author of the *Short Account of Porson*, and to John Matthews by Moore, *Life of Byron* (1832), II, p. 40.

Porson of the charge of writing *Eloisa en Dishabille*, it does not imply a vindication of his taste, for he was notoriously fond of reciting the profligate parody.

Some of Porson's lesser productions eventually found their way into print; a good number were published in Beloe's *Sexagenarian*, and some were included in such collections as *Facetiae Cantabrigienses* and *The Cambridge Tart*. Others remained unprinted and are now irrecoverable. We hear of 'a severe satire on a royal duke, which was very properly suppressed',[1] and nothing is now known of his satire on the Seniors of Trinity, then notorious for their immoral manner of life, except the four lines which are all that Gunning ventures to quote. These concern the Rev. William Backhouse, B.D., who 'instituted a school for females, in the management of which he was much censured':

> Was it profit that he sought?
> No: he paid them to be taught.
> Had he honour for his aim?
> No: he *blush'd to find it fame*.[2]

One more activity of Porson's, though not exactly literary, may be mentioned here. He delighted all his life in calligraphy, and would spend many hours in the exercise of writing both in English and Greek. His transcript of Photius has already been mentioned; he transcribed also two complete plays of Euripides, the *Medea* and the *Phoenissae*, which like the Photius are in the library of Trinity. The Photius was intended for publication, but the utilitarian value of these transcriptions was out of proportion to the care he expended on

[1] Gordon, *Personal Memoirs*, I, p. 287.
[2] Gunning, *Reminiscences of Cambridge*, II, p. 114.

them. He derived a real pleasure from the mere writing of Greek.

His English handwriting is not in the highest class. It developed little since his schooldays at Happisburgh, and always showed the influence of the country writing-master. Compared with the bold scholarly hand of some of his foreign contemporaries, Hermann for instance, it appears weak and lacking in character. It is marked by neatness and fineness, and was legible even when, as it pleased him sometimes to do, he wrote in minutely small characters.

His particular interest was in Greek script. Here his qualities of neatness and clearness were particularly valuable as a model for printers.[1] We hear of his association with the type-founder Vincent Figgins,[2] and also with Richard Austin, who, assisted by Richard Watts, cut under Porson's supervision the famous Greek type that bears his name.[3] This 'Great Porson Greek' was adopted by the Cambridge Press after his death, being first used in 1810 for Blomfield's *Prometheus*. In 1826 it was used for the collected edition of Porson's own four plays of Euripides, published by Scholefield, the Greek professor of that day.

Porson experimented with various scripts, as his manuscripts show, but the general tendency of his writing was towards simplicity and clarity, and the type adopted by the Cambridge Press has for many years proved

[1] He contributed the abbreviations to Hodgkin's *Calligraphia et Poikilographia Graeca* (1807). The Greek script recommended by Hodgkin was that of Dr Young, and could hardly have met with Porson's approval.

[2] T. B. Reed, *History of the Old English Letter Foundries*, p. 342.

[3] Wordsworth, *Scholae Academicae*, p. 392.

serviceable and agreeable for ordinary use. We may quote a criticism of it by Mr Victor Scholderer, the designer of the 'New Hellenic' type, which has recently to some extent supplanted Porson's.

'The lower case is of simple, even and legible design, well rounded and entirely without ligatures and contractions, and constitutes a much more definite break with tradition than any of its immediate predecessors. Unfortunately it still retains the slope characteristic of post-Aldine Greek—a matter in which its originator was no doubt influenced by his own rather excessively sloping pen-script—and this alone would effectively exclude it from the highest class of Greek letter, even if the capitals, which are upright, had much more distinction than is actually the case. Nevertheless the Porson Greek as a whole marks a very great step forward.... Greek printing in England, especially the standard types adopted by the University Presses of Oxford and Cambridge, had but to follow Porson's lead to rank as the best in contemporary Europe.'[1]

[1] Scholderer, *Greek Printing Types*, p. 14.

Aristophanes Plut. 134. 144.

Καὶ νὴ Δί; εὔχονται γε πλουτεῖν ἀντικρυς·
Καὶ νὴ Δί; εἴ τι γ᾽ἐστι λαμπρὸν καὶ καλόν.

Ubi Mst. Dorvillii ἔνεστι habet, frustra probatum a Koeni-
o ad Gregorium p. 18. Neque tamen hilum interest, horace-
datne particula, an subsequatur.

Aristophanes Plut. 1022.

Εἰ Θάσιον ἔνεχεῖς, εἰκότως γε, νὴ Δία.

Equit. 937.

Εὖ γε νὴ τὸν Δία καὶ τὸν Ἀπόλλω.

Sic enim legi debet pro Εὖ νή γε τὸν — ex tribus Brunckii
Mst. editione Juntina a. 1515. et Scholiaste. Quod autem diax particulam γε non hoc juᵍⁱⁿᵃᵐⁱmento postpo-
ni, nisi interjecta alia voce, idem de καὶ μὴν — γε et
οὐ μὴν — γε dictum puta.

Sophocles Oedipo Tyr. 981.

Καὶ μὴν μέγας γ᾽ὀφθαλμὸς οἱ πατρὸς τάφοι.

ἐσθ᾽ τόδε habet·
v. χάριν.

FACSIMILE OF PORSON'S HANDWRITING, INCLUDING GREEK CHARACTERS

VIII

As Regius professor, Porson paid a yearly visit to his University for the purpose of examining. But it is likely enough that he stayed there longer than was required by his duties. Though not a Fellow he had rooms and commons at Trinity by virtue of his professorship, and we gain the impression that he was a not unfamiliar figure in Cambridge in the latter part of this life. After Postlethwaite's death in 1798 Porson perhaps felt more at ease in his college, and we may suppose that he gradually lost his sense of grievance against the University.

Towards the end of his life he made some new friends at Cambridge. One of these was a young man from Guernsey, Peter Paul Dobree, who was to carry on the Porsonian tradition of scholarship with something approaching Porson's felicity. In May 1805 Burney wrote to Porson: 'If you can, see, and take good notice of a young friend of mine of Trinity College named Dobree.'[1] Porson followed this advice, and Dobree became an intimate friend as well as a disciple of his.[2]

Another new friend was the versatile traveller E. D. Clarke, of Jesus, who brought back from his travels inscriptions and manuscripts that were naturally a source of delight to the Greek professor. Clarke has given his impressions of Porson, whom he first met early in

---

[1] *Correspondence*, p. 105.
[2] See his memorial in Trinity College Chapel, and his praelection.

1802. 'I had seen him at my rooms in the morning, and we bore off together to Trinity the Plato and the Aulus Gellius. In the evening he came already primed, and did not miss fire. He was great indeed, narrating, reciting, sometimes full of fun and laughing: at others weeping bitterly at the sufferings of friends that flourished near 2000 years ago, but with whom he seemed as well acquainted and as familiar as if they had smoked a pipe with him the preceding evening. At about three in the morning a curtain seemed all at once to fall over his mind; ale, wine and smoke had extinguished the intellectual flame, and he remained from that moment until he left me, like the beam of some great building on fire, whose flame the engines have put out, black and reeking.'[1]

At Cambridge, Porson was familiar with undergraduates, and when they were impertinent threatened them with a poker. Once one of them seized the tongs in reply. 'If I should crack your skull,' said Porson, 'I believe I should find it empty.' 'And if I should crack yours,' answered the young man, 'I should find it full of maggots.' Porson, pleased with the retort, laid down the poker with a smile and repeated a chapter of *Roderick Random* suitable to the occasion.

This use of the poker was notorious, for Byron mentions it in the very unfavourable account of Porson he gives in a letter to Murray. According to him the professor was sober in hall and combination room, but in private parties always drunk or brutal, and generally both. 'I have seen Sheridan drunk too with all the world; but his intoxication was that of Bacchus, and Porson's that of Silenus. Of all the disgusting brutes,

[1] Otter, *Life of Clarke*, p. 560.

[78]

sulky, abusive and intolerable, Porson was the most bestial as far as the few times that I saw him went, which were only at William Bankes's (the Nubian Discoverer's) rooms. I saw him once go away in a rage because nobody knew the name of the 'Cobbler of Messina', insulting their ignorance with the most vulgar terms of reprobation. He was tolerated in this state amongst the young men for his talents, as the Turks think a madman inspired and bear with him. He used to recite or rather vomit pages of all languages, and could hiccup Greek like a Helot: and certainly Sparta never shocked her children with a grosser exhibition than this man's intoxication.'[1]

Byron, who was at Cambridge from 1805 to 1807, saw Porson in his decline, when he was beginning to pay the penalty for his self-indulgence. It was not surprising that an impressionable young man should find him disgusting. But that Porson in 1807 could appear in more attractive guise to an undergraduate is shown by a letter of T. S. Hughes, in which he recalls, nearly twenty years later, an interview with Porson in his tutor's rooms. More balanced and tolerant than Byron's, his account deserves to be quoted at length.

'After about an hour spent in various subjects of conversation, during which the Professor recited a great many beautiful passages from authors in Greek, Latin, French and English, my tutor, seeing the visitation that was evidently intended for him, feigned an excuse for going into the town, and left Porson and myself together. I ought to have observed that he had already produced one bottle of sherry to moisten the Professor's throat, and that he left out another, in case it should be required.

---

[1] Moore, *Life of Byron*, Letter 308.

Porson's spirits being by this time elevated by the juice of the grape, and being pleased with a well-timed compliment which I had the good luck to address to him, he became very communicative; said he was glad that we had met together; desired me to take up my pen and paper, and directed me to write down, from his dictation, many curious algebraical problems, with their solutions; gave me several ingenious methods of summing series; and ran through a great variety of the properties of numbers.

'After almost an hour's occupation in this manner, he said, "Lay aside your pen, and listen to the history of a man of letters,—how he became a sordid miser from a thoughtless prodigal, a .... from a ...., and a misanthrope from a morbid excess of sensibility." (I forget the intermediate step in the climax.) He then commenced a narrative of his own life, from his entrance at Eton school, through all the most remarkable periods, to the day of our conversation. I was particularly amused with the account of his school anecdotes, the tricks he used to play on his master and schoolfellows, and the little dramatic pieces which he wrote for private representation. From these he passed to his academical pursuits and studies, his election to the Greek professorship, and his ejection from his fellowship through the influence of Dr Postlethwaite, who, though he had promised it to Porson, exerted it for a relation of his own. "I was then", said the Professor, 'almost destitute in the wide world, with less than 40 l. a year for my support, and without a profession, for I never could bring myself to subscribe Articles of Faith. I used often to lie awake through the whole night, and wish for a large pearl."

'He then gave me the history of his life in London, when he took chambers in the Temple, and read at times immoderately hard. He very much interested me by a curious interview which he had with a girl of the town, who came into his chambers by mistake, and who showed so much cleverness and ability in a long conversation with him, that he declared she might with proper cultivation have become another Aspasia. He also recited to me, word for word, the speech with which he accosted Dr Postlethwaite when he called at his chambers, and which he had long prepared against such an occurrence. At the end of this oration the Doctor said not a word, but burst into tears and left the room. Porson also burst into tears when he finished the recital of it to me.

'In this manner five hours passed away; at the end of which the Professor, who had finished the second bottle of my friend's sherry, began to clip the King's English, to cry like a child at the close of his periods, and in other respects to show marks of extreme debility. At length he rose from his chair, staggered to the door, and made his way downstairs without taking the slightest notice of his companion. I retired to my college and next morning was informed by my friend that he had been out upon a search the previous evening for the Greek Professor, whom he discovered near the outskirts of the town, leaning upon the arm of a dirty bargeman, and amusing him by the most humorous and laughable anecdotes.'[1]

Dons, undergraduates, even bargemen, enjoyed Porson's company; he was also, like some other men of great intellectual powers, fond of children, and could

[1] *Correspondence*, p. 133; Watson, *Life of Porson*, p. 385.

gratify this taste among the numerous offspring of Thomas Verney Okes, a Cambridge surgeon. Richard, the nineteenth child of the family, who later became Provost of King's, and still held this office within living memory, was one of Porson's favourites. In later life he would recall a curious incident of his childhood. He was at home with his brothers and sisters doing lessons, learning the verb 'rego', I rule. Porson came in, presumably not quite sober, wrote up on the board: 'Rego, I draw a straight line, Regis, thou drawst a straight line', etc., and then left the room.[1]

For the last two years of his life, Porson was for the first time in comfortable circumstances. On April 23, 1806, he was elected principal librarian of the London Institution, which had just been founded, and was then situated in Old Jewry.[2] His new office brought him a salary of £200, with a set of rooms and a servant. The distinction of his name no doubt brought honour to the Institution, but as a librarian he was not a great success, and the Directors in a letter to him complained that 'we only know you are our librarian by seeing your name attached to the receipts for your salary'. His neglect of his duties was in part excused by his ill-health; the asthma from which he had suffered for some years was getting worse, and a rooted prejudice made him refuse to seek medical aid. His habits were still irregular, and his appearance shabby. Hazlitt saw him once at the London Institution, 'dressed in an old rusty black coat with cobwebs hanging to the skirts of it, and with a large patch of coarse brown paper covering the whole

[1] A. C. Benson, *Fasti Etonenses*, p. 235.
[2] In 1819 it moved to Finsbury Circus, and in 1912 it ceased to exist. Its buildings became the School of Oriental Studies.

length of his nose, looking for all the world like a drunken carpenter, and talking to one of the proprietors with an air of suavity, approaching to condescension'.[1]

In February of 1806 he went up to Cambridge to vote for the Whig, Lord Henry Petty, who took Pitt's place as Member for the University.[2] In August of the same year he paid his last visit to his sister at Coltishall, and while he was there went over to his native village for the funeral of his father, old Huggin Porson, who died on September 8. He himself survived his father only two years.

On September 19, 1808, he left his rooms at the London Institution to visit his brother-in-law in the Strand. Perry was not in, and Porson walked on, but had not gone far when he was seized with an apoplectic fit, and was found speechless and helpless in the street. There was no means of identifying him, and he was taken to a neighbouring workhouse to spend the night. The authorities inserted a description of him in the papers the next morning, mentioning 'the memorandum book, the leaves of which were filled chiefly with Greek lines written with a pencil, and partly effaced, two or three lines of Latin, and an algebraical calculation'. James Savage, one of the officials of the Institution, recognised that this must be the professor and went to fetch him back. He seemed to have recovered to some extent, and conversed intelligently as they drove to Old Jewry. As they passed St Paul's he spoke feelingly of Sir Christopher Wren and the ill-treatment he had received in the latter part of his life.

After breakfasting at his rooms on green tea and toast

[1] Hazlitt, *Table Talk*. On Coffee House Politicians.
[2] Genest, *Some Account of the English Stage*, x, p. 264.

he went to the library, and there met Dr Adam Clarke, who has left an account of the meeting. Porson looked extremely ill, and spoke with difficulty. In a low voice he repeated more than once, 'I have just escaped death'. They proceeded to discuss Greek inscriptions, and Porson, in spite of the pain that speaking caused him, seemed anxious to continue the conversation. Dr Clarke noted in particular how after quoting a Greek couplet with comparative ease, he found great difficulty in uttering an English translation of it. 'The truth is,' remarks Clarke, 'so imbued was his mind with Grecian literature that he thought as well as spoke in that language, and found it much more easy at this time, from the power of habit and association, than to pronounce his mother tongue.'

As if anxious not to give way to his weakness, Porson followed his visitor to the top of the stairs, and continued to talk leaning over the balustrade, and a little later went out himself to take his dinner at a favourite coffeehouse. There he arrived in a state of great weakness, unable to eat and scarcely able to speak. He could only repeat in a low voice again and again: 'The gentleman said it was a ludicrous piece of business, and I think so too.' He was taken back to the Institution and with difficulty persuaded to go to bed. Doctors were summoned, but nothing could now be done to save him, and after a few days he died. His body was transferred to Cambridge, where, on October 3, it was buried with every mark of sorrow and respect in the chapel of his college.

IX

To Thomas Kidd, Porson seemed gentle, religious, unworldly, the possessor of every virtue, or to be accurate, of every virtue but one, for even Kidd could not shut his eyes to Porson's intemperance. To Byron, on the other hand, he was merely a disgusting brute. The truth, it need hardly be said, was somewhere between the two extremes, but of the two witnesses Byron was the blinder. Porson was in his way a great man, for there was about him something of that quality of uniqueness that justifies this title. It is unfortunate that none of those who came under his spell had the skill or the desire to transmit his personality to those who never knew him. The anecdotes of his contemporaries give us, to quote the title of a biographical pamphlet, mere 'scraps from Porson's rich feast'.

Porson was ill served by his contemporaries. The literary men of the '80's and '90's with whom he came in contact were an undistinguished lot; the more important men lived away from London, or took no interest in Porson. Consequently he remains in some obscurity. Bentley had the distinction of being attacked by Swift and Pope, and his books engaged the attention of the whole literary world. Porson left no such mark on English literature, for one would hardly compare *The Pursuits of Literature* with the *Dunciad*.

Porson's character was admittedly not perfect. We need not dwell on his drunkenness. His contemporaries regarded it on the whole with tolerance, and such weaknesses endear the great to posterity. He lacked the gift of temperance, and there were other minor virtues in which he was deficient. He was not always cleanly or polite, nor was his tongue always free from malice. His μνησικακία against Postlethwaite may seem to some to show an unamiable quality. But the main features of his character deserve our admiration. As C. J. Blomfield said: 'He had two qualities that are essential requisites in the formation of a great character,—an utter contempt for money, and a religious devotion to truth.'[1] And Dobree in the tribute to Porson with which he began his praelection as Greek professor, said: 'His character was simple, upright, noble and undaunted. In everything he was so eager for truth, so firmly devoted to honesty, that his friends were wont to regard him as a model of honesty and good faith. His contempt for money, honours, and what are commonly thought goods was utterly genuine, and he considered nothing in this world as his concern except the consciousness of right and the advancement of literature.'[2]

Porson's friends admired his indifference to money. We have seen how he described himself as having become a sordid miser from a thoughtless prodigal, and strangely enough there seems to be something in this confession, for when he died he was found to have left property of over £3000. It is true that about two-thirds of this was accounted for by his library, the value of which was doubtless increased by his ownership, but even so it remains a mystery how he accumulated so much when his income until his last two years was only about £140. Perhaps his editions of Euripides were

[1] *Museum Criticum*, I, 397.
[2] Dobree, *Adversaria*, I, p. 5 (translated).

more profitable than we should expect, or there was some other source of income which we do not know of. At any rate it is unlikely that he spent much except on books and drink. He was as indifferent to food as to sleep, and could always go without a meal if he wished.

His whole career shows his lack of ambition. This may be admired as disinterestedness or condemned as indolence, but whether rightly or wrongly Porson never desired worldly honour or fame. If he had, he could probably have won it in any of the careers then open. Ordination might have brought promotion, though it was a bad period for Whigs, and Parr all his life sighed in vain for what he called 'the profits and splendour of the prelacy'. But even outside the episcopate there were (to use Gaisford's famous words) 'places of emolument and dignity', to which a knowledge of Greek (combined with holy orders) might lead. But Porson had no desire for dignity or emolument, and his devotion to the truth as he saw it forbade him to take holy orders.

Whether he could have attained fame in other fields is not a very profitable speculation. He cannot in imagination be suitably fitted to the world of politics, except in the region where it adjoins that of literature and journalism, the region where Swift exercised his biting pen. Porson's irony is a mild affair compared with that of Swift, and his journalism never extended beyond a single pamphlet and some ephemeral pieces for the daily press. But whatever his capacities, his inclinations never led him far outside the realms of classical scholarship. He could lampoon his contemporaries effectively, and in literature could ridicule impostors and second-rate performers, and even criticise the giants, such as Gibbon;

[87]

but, though with more ambition he might have won a greater position in the literary life of the day, he was conscious of an incapacity for original composition on a considerable scale.

Somebody once asked him why he produced so little original work. Porson answered: 'I doubt if I could produce any original work that would command the attention of posterity. I can be known only by my notes; and I am quite satisfied if, 300 years hence, it shall be said that one Porson lived towards the close of the eighteenth century who did a good deal for the text of Euripides.' Again, we hear of him exclaiming with tears in his eyes: 'Why should I write from myself, while anything remains to be done to such a writer as Euripides?'[1] We are reminded of Bentley, who similarly excused himself for not giving himself to original composition. 'The wit and genius of those old heathens beguiled me: and as I despaired of raising myself up to their standard upon fair ground, I thought the only chance I had of looking over their heads was to get upon their shoulders.'[2]

Porson's ambition was limited, and so were his achievements, but his interests were by no means confined to the narrow field of Greek drama. E. D. Clarke after meeting him wrote: 'All the accounts I have heard of this wonderful man for so many years have not raised my expectations high enough to see him without astonishment. Τοῦ καὶ ἀπὸ γλώσσης μέλιτος γλυκίων ῥέεν αὐδή. So rare is it to find among men the highest attainments in ancient literature, joined to a love of the poetry of yesterday, the most refined genius and almost

[1] Rogers, *Recollections*, p. 121.
[2] Quoted by Jebb, *Life of Bentley*, p. 209.

supernatural intellect.'[1] Similarly, Hazlitt excepted
Porson from his general attack on learned pedants. 'He
was an exception that confirmed the general rule—a man
that by uniting talents and knowledge with learning,
made the distinction between them more striking and
palpable.'[2]

Hazlitt did not know Porson personally, and may have
been prejudiced in his favour by his political views.
De Quincey, who knew him equally little, was as a Tory
prejudiced against him. Porson according to him read
no poetry at all 'unless it were either political or
obscene'.[3] This is certainly untrue. His frequent quotations, though they may have included the political and
the obscene, included much else besides. He had a wide
and intimate knowledge of English literature, and a
special love of Shakespeare. Among his manuscripts are
to be found some notes on passages of Shakespeare, and
certain marginal comments of his on English writers
show the same learning and incisiveness that he applied
to Greek. His literary tastes were sure and normal;
besides Shakespeare he admired Milton, Pope and Swift.
He enjoyed polemical and anti-Governmental writing,
from the *Letters of Junius* to the tracts of Thomas
Gordon, the Whig and anti-clerical pamphleteer.

Porson's literary interests and tastes were of the
eighteenth century. We do not know what he thought of
the new poets who emerged in the latter part of his life.
De Quincey was probably right in believing that he
never met Wordsworth or read any of his poetry;
Landor's dialogue, in which Porson and Southey discuss

[1] Otter, *Life of Clarke*, p. 560.
[2] Hazlitt, *Table Talk*. On the Ignorance of the Learned.
[3] De Quincey, *Works* (ed. Masson), XI, p. 417.

[89]

Wordsworth's writing, is wholly imaginary. On Southey Porson made a characteristic pronouncement: 'Mr Southey is indeed a wonderful writer; his works will be read when Homer and Virgil are forgotten.' Which Byron, to avoid all possible misapprehension, quoted with the addition of 'but not till then'.

Porson was unusually well read in French literature, and he once remarked that if he had a son he would try to make him familiar with French and English authors; Greek and Latin were only luxuries. He confessed to having a very strong prejudice against all German original literature; but it has been confidently stated that he knew no German. About his acquaintance with Italian there is some doubt; Maltby states that he knew little or none, but Pryse Gordon has an anecdote in which Porson reads an Italian novel and translates it from memory.

In Greek his favourite authors were Aristophanes and the tragedians; but if we may believe Monk his real love was Athenaeus, whom he studied closely for thirty years.[1] In the Deipnosophists, who conversed learnedly and quoted extensively over their wine, he recognised perhaps congenial spirits, and in their fragments of poetry he found plenty of scope for his skill in emendation. Of Thucydides we are told he knew comparatively little, and he did not greatly care for Lucian. Latin literature did not interest him much, though he was fond of Cicero, especially of the Tusculan Disputations, and he thought it worth while to quote, in his editions of Euripides, the versions of the Latin tragedians.

To T. S. Hughes, Porson described himself as having become a misanthrope from an excess of sensibility.

[1] Letter of Monk to Butler, Add. MSS. 34,583, f. 381.

Those who knew him but slightly saw only the outer mask of the misanthrope, and not the Man of Feeling beneath. Sensibility was a fashionable quality at the time, and Porson certainly had a share of it, as was shown by the way in which he took the loss of his Fellowship, and by the tears to be seen in his eyes when he was moved. We are told that 'when repeating a generous action from antiquity or describing a death like Phocion's, his eyes would fill and his voice falter'.[1] And tears were to be seen rolling down his cheeks as he recited some moving poem.[2]

Bentley could write the Boyle lectures as well as the *Dissertation on Phalaris* and the editions of Latin poets, but textual critics have not for the most part been greatly interested in philosophy or abstract thought. Porson was no exception. 'With all your learning,' said Parr once to him, 'I do not think you well versed in metaphysics'; to which Porson answered, 'I suppose you mean your metaphysics.' But it was true that he was not 'well versed in metaphysics'. His only excursion into theology was into a question of criticism, and the interest in Plato which he discovered towards the end of his life was probably textual rather than philosophical.

For his chosen work he was admirably equipped by nature. His memory was famous in his day, and anecdotes concerning it are still current. His own account of himself is rather a paradox. 'Anyone might become as good a critic as I am, if he would only take the trouble

---

[1] Rogers, *Recollections*, p. 121.

[2] The two works that are mentioned as having thus moved him are the Chorus in *Hercules Furens* beginning Ἀ νεότης μοι φίλον ἄχθος (637f.) and Pope's *Epistle to the Earl of Oxford* prefixed to Parnell's poems.

to make himself so. I have made myself what I am by intense labour; sometimes in order to impress a thing on my memory I have read it a dozen times and transcribed it six.' Porson had no desire to lay claim to any peculiar gifts, but he does not convince us that hard work is all that is required to become a Porson. What of the 'divinandi quaedam peritia et μαντικὴ', that faculty which according to Bentley cannot be acquired by toil or long life, but is the gift of nature? Porson certainly had something of this, less no doubt than Bentley had, but better disciplined and consequently less dangerous. 'Bentley's faculty for discovering the truth', wrote Housman, 'has no equal in the history of learning, but his wish to discover it was not so strong. Critics like Porson and Lachmann, inferior in εὐστοχία and ἀγχίνοια, put him to shame by their serious and disinterested purpose and the honesty of their dealings with themselves.'[1] To sum up those gifts of intellect and character which Porson brought to classical scholarship we may borrow the admirable words of Jebb: 'He brought extraordinary gifts and absolute fidelity to his chosen province, leaving work most important in its positive and permanent results, but remarkable above all for its quality—the quality given to it by his individual genius, by that powerful and penetrating mind, at once brilliant and patient, serious and sportive by turns, but in every mood devoted with a scrupulous loyalty to the search for truth.'[2]

To us to-day Porson's scholarship may seem narrow and limited, a matter of a few happy emendations and some metrical discoveries. But his range was wider than

[1] *Manilius*, I, p. xviii.
[2] *Dictionary of National Biography*, art. Richard Porson, *ad fin.*

this. Like many of his contemporaries he was interested in inscriptions. At one time he was often to be seen in the British Museum studying the Rosetta Stone, whose mutilated Greek inscription he was able to restore and explain. When E. D. Clarke published his *Dissertation on the Sarcophagus brought from Alexandria*, Porson wrote to him supplying much relevant information.[1] He was at home with manuscripts as well as with inscriptions, and found much to interest him in Clarke's collection. In particular, the Plato from Patmos occupied his attention, and he constantly had it with him during the last years of his life. He was no stranger to the minute labour of collating manuscripts, or to the lengthy, though to him congenial, task of transcription. He had a good practical acquaintance with manuscripts and a sense of their value and limitations; he cannot be accused of ignoring their evidence, nor would he ever have uttered the arrogant words: 'Nobis et ratio et res ipsa centum codicibus potiores sunt.'

But we must not commend Porson's learning on false grounds. Bywater in an Oxford lecture remarked that 'when advice was wanted on a matter connected with the Herculaneum papyri, Tyrwhitt declared that Porson was the only man in England qualified to give an opinion'.[2] Very likely he was, but the man who said so was not qualified to judge, for it was not Thomas Tyrwhitt the scholar, who had been dead for some years, but his nephew of the same name, a court official and a patron of learning, but not, so far as we know, a scholar.

[1] Otter, *Life of Clarke*, p. 547.
[2] Bywater, *Four Centuries of Classical Learning* (in Oxford Lectures on Classical Subjects), p. 18. Cf. Porson, *Correspondence*, p. 104.

In mere erudition Porson was probably surpassed by his contemporaries Parr and Burney, both of them famous for their extensive libraries. Porson's learning was no doubt considerable, but it was not prominently displayed. His notes are brief, and concerned chiefly with the text. Like Bentley in his *Horace* and Housman in his *Manilius* he left to others the task of illustrating the subject matter. 'Interpretandi et illustrandi labore, utilissimo sane, supersedendum duxi, partim ne libellus in librum cresceret.'[1] The lengthy note near the beginning of his *Orestes*, in which he illustrates the story of Tantalus by a number of quotations from various authors, was apparently a half-humorous answer to those like Wakefield who objected to the spareness of his notes. It showed what he could do in this style of annotation, but that it was not to be taken quite seriously was shown by his remark towards the end of the note: 'Nescio, benevole lector, an tuam patientiam hac nota legenda fatigaris; meam certe scribenda fatigavi.' But sometimes in conversation Porson would display his fund of apt commentary, and illustrate a favourite author, Aristophanes for example, with a learning and wit that his listeners did not soon forget, and Dobree thought it worth while to recall the admiration aroused by his translations into English.[2]

The reputation of Parr as a scholar has slumped badly, and that of Burney is lower than it once was, but Porson's reputation remains as high as ever. A. E. Housman, the man in our day best qualified to judge, gave his assent to the general opinion in this country that places him second to Bentley among English

[1] Preface to *Hecuba, ad fin.*
[2] Dobree, *Adversaria*, I, p. 6.

scholars.[1] Porson, when he hoped to be remembered for his notes 300 years later, was anticipating a long life for classical studies. Half that period has not yet elapsed, but so far his modest ambition may be said to have been achieved. His name is to be seen attached to many accepted emendations. His metrical canons have been incorporated in the text-books, and many generations have learned them at school without knowing that they were Porson's. Learnt early and taken for granted, they have formed the basis of the sound metrical sense that has distinguished most Greek scholars of this country.

[1] *Classical Review*, xxxiv, p. 111.

X

AT the head of the classical scholarship of the eighteenth
century stands the figure of Richard Bentley, and like
his digamma, o'ertops them all. It was he who turned
scholarship from the antiquarianism of the seventeenth
century to the work of freeing the texts from corruption,
and this work was the main business of his followers.
But whereas Bentley had in later life kept chiefly to
Latin, the best scholars of the eighteenth century after
Bentley devoted themselves for the most part to Greek.
It was not the Bentley of the *Horace* or the *Manilius*, or
even of the *Dissertation on Phalaris* who marked out the
way for succeeding scholars, but rather the Bentley
of the *Letter to Mill*. In that early work he projected
a collection of fragments of all the Greek poets with
emendations and notes, and at about the same time he
was planning an edition of the most important Greek
lexica. The same interest in the ancient lexica can be
seen in the transcriber of Photius and annotator of
Toup's *Suidas*, the same love of emending fragments
in the scholar who enjoyed few ancient writers more
than Athenaeus. Porson trod in his own manner where
Bentley had pointed the way. His admiration for the
great critic was well known; he used to say that when
he was seventeen he thought he knew everything, but
when he was twenty-four and had read Bentley he
realised that he knew nothing; and it is recorded that
he wept tears of joy on discovering that some of his
emendations had been anticipated by Bentley, showing

a generous emotion that not all scholars feel on such occasions.

By the side of the great Master of Trinity we may place the obscure figure of an unsuccessful northern schoolmaster. Second only to Bentley in Porson's esteem was Richard Dawes, whose *Miscellanea Critica* was one of the most popular works of scholarship of the eighteenth century, and went through five editions between 1745 and 1827. It is not without significance that two editions were called for in the early nineteenth century, during the period of the 'Porsonian school'. It was Dawes who first attempted by means of accurate and laborious observation of Attic usage to fix laws of diction and syntax. He is chiefly known for a canon which has not been generally accepted, but many of his other observations have become part of our common knowledge, and though he was not always cautious enough in enouncing his laws, scholars certainly owed to him a sharpening of their grammatical perceptions.

Dawes proposed many Aristophanic emendations in the course of his *Miscellanea Critica*. Other scholars of the same period, Heath, Musgrave, Markland, edited the Attic dramatists and emended them with some success. But much remained to be done. The texts were still presented with many corruptions. Porson applied himself to the same problems that had exercised his predecessors, and by his combination of brilliance and carefulness set a new standard to his younger contemporaries.

We have attempted to show that Porson's interests were by no means narrow, but it must be admitted that his fruitful labours were almost entirely confined to a small field, that of Attic drama. Even there the choral lyrics fell outside his scope. It is primarily as a textual critic and a metrist that he is remembered.

Textual criticism is a pursuit that gives amusement and satisfaction to its practitioners, and to others who can appreciate without practising; it will be admitted, too, that it allows for the exercise of rare intellectual qualities. It will be less readily admitted that there are not more worthy objects for the exercise of the intellect. The textual critic did not reign unchallenged in Porson's day, when there was more scope than there is now for useful exercise in this field. Porson himself is said to have projected a defence of verbal scholarship, but like other projects of his, this came to nothing. In default of any utterance of his own we may refer to some words of Payne Knight, which he quoted with evident approval.

After complaining of the injustice by which the aesthetic critic is ranked with the orator and the historian, while the textual critic is 'degraded with the index-maker and antiquary', Knight proceeds: 'But, nevertheless, if we examine the effects produced by these two classes of Criticks, we shall find that the first have been of no use whatever, and that the last have rendered important services to mankind. All persons of taste and understanding know, from their own feelings, when to approve, and disapprove, and therefore stand in no need of instructions from the Critick; and as for those who are destitute of such faculties, they can never be taught to use them; for no one can be taught to exert faculties which he does not possess.... But whatever be the taste and discernment of a reader, or the genius and ability of a writer, neither the one nor the other can appear while the text remains deformed by the corruptions of blundering transcribers, and obscured by the glosses of ignorant grammarians. It is then that the aid of the verbal critic is required; and though his minute labour in dissecting syllables and analysing letters may appear contemptible in its operation, it will be found important in its effect.'[1]

Whether his work was worth doing or not, Porson certainly did it well. His textual criticism is not marred by those faults that bring the art into disrepute. He does not alter capriciously to satisfy his own taste or to show his disagreement with other scholars. He does not indulge in the brilliant improvisations of Bentley. Every emendation must be shown to be necessary, must be supported by parallels, and referred if possible to some general rule of style. 'Nihil contemnendum est, neque in bello neque in re critica.'[2]

Porson can commend his comments by the good sense and economy with which he makes them. Those who were familiar with the commentaries of the period admired the freshness and clarity of his Latin style. They enjoyed the veiled references to Wakefield and Hermann, the confidential addresses to 'adulescentes optimi', and the quaint humour with which, for instance, he embarks upon a long and irrelevant note: 'Nihil enim maius habemus quod agamus, et otio fruimur.' In his Appendix to Toup's *Suidas* he had protested against the cant that overloaded classical notes with words of praise, 'pulchre, bene, recte, etc.', and though he gives credit where it is due, he avoids these conventional eulogies. Adverbs of censure are equally rare, for generally he prefers the method of ironical commendation, and when

[1] Quoted in review of Knight's *Essay on the Greek Alphabet*, *Tracts and Criticisms*, p. 109.
[2] Porson on *Medea*, 139.

confuting some erroneous opinion calls its author 'vir summus' or 'egregius', or if he has convicted him of a metrical blunder, 'vir metri callentissimus'. The extent of our debt to Porson may be judged by the number of accepted emendations in our texts to which his name is attached. Many of these are useful unspectacular corrections. It is inevitable, though perhaps wrong, that the neat and ingenious emendations should arouse most admiration, as that of *Agamemnon* 1391 (χαίρουσαν οὐδὲν ἧσσον ἢ διοσδότῳ γάνει σπορητὸς κάλυκος ἐν λοχεύμασιν for... ἢ Διὸς νότῳ γᾶν, εἰ σπορητὸς...) or of *Helen* 751 (Κάλχας γὰρ οὐκ εἶπ' οὐδ' ἐσήμηνε στρατῷ νεφέλης ὑπερθνήσκοντας εἰσορῶν φίλους, οὐδ' Ἕλενος... for οὐδέν γε).

Most famous perhaps of all his emendations is that of *Ion* 1115. There the MSS. read ἐγνώσμεθ' ἐξ ἴσου κἂν ὑστάτοις κακοῖς.[1] Modern texts print a correction due to Porson, ἔγνως· μεθέξεις δ' οὐκ ἐν ὑστάτοις κακοῦ, which makes good sense, and keeps almost exactly to the letters of the MSS. It is one of those emendations that appear obvious once they have been given currency, and to appreciate how little obvious it was one must look at the bungling efforts of earlier scholars, as recorded in some old Variorum edition. The word δ', which is considered necessary to the line, is attributed, rightly enough, to Hermann; and Porson was censured by Housman for being seduced into omitting the necessary particle by an anxious adherence to the *ductus litterarum*.[2] But it is by no means certain that this charge is justified. Porson's emendation was originally published (without the δ') in Kidd's notes to his edition of Dawes's

---

[1] Or so it was believed. In fact L. has κἐν.
[2] Housman, *Manilius*, v, p. xxxv.

Miscellanea Critica.[1] Dindorf called attention to it, and Hermann adopted it, with the addition of the particle. Hermann's edition of the *Ion* is dated 1827, and in the same year appeared Kidd's second edition of Dawes, with the δ' tacitly added in his note.[2] Now it is improbable that Kidd, a schoolmaster in a small country town, could have obtained Hermann's *Ion* before his own book went to press, unless Hermann sent him a copy,[3] nor is it likely that, being a man of simple goodness, he would have committed the minor deceit of attributing to Porson what was due to another. It is at least not improbable that he was simply correcting an error in his first edition, and that Porson himself had seen the necessity of the particle.

One cannot always judge of a scholar's merits from the number of times his name appears in an *apparatus criticus*. Often a later editor gets the credit, when he merely improves where another has shown the way. For instance in Ar. *Ach.* 645, where the MSS. have ὅστις παρεκινδύνευσεν 'Αθηναίοις εἰπεῖν τὰ δίκαια, the Oxford text prints Hermann's ὅστις παρεκινδύνευσ' εἰπεῖν ἐν 'Αθηναίοις τὰ δίκαια. This may be better than Porson's ὅστις γ' εἰπεῖν παρεκινδύνευσ' ἐν 'Αθηναίοις τὰ δίκαια, but it was he who noticed the absence of caesura, and saw the preposition lurking at the end of the verb.[4]

One of Porson's favourite occupations, one which must have given him especial satisfaction, was the correction of those fragments of poetry which have been preserved in a confused and corrupt state by ancient lexicographers or by miscellaneous writers like Athe-

---

[1] (1817), p. 293. [2] P. 299.
[3] His Preface is dated May 1827. I do not know at what time of the year Hermann's book appeared
[4] Suppl. ad Praef. *Hec.* p. 46.

naeus. Watch him in one or two such cases produce order out of chaos, and judge what must be the intellectual pleasure of solving such problems.

Hesychius has under Παλινδορία (a kind of leather) the following remark: Πλάτων Σύρφακι καὶ Μωμοθήρᾳ. παλινδορία παίσας αὐτοῦ καταθήσω, or according to another manuscript Πλάτων συρφακίσαι, μνωμοχθῆραι; and from the former reading a play Μωμοθήρας had been attributed to Plato. Porson reads: Πλάτων Σύρφακι· Σὲ μὲν, ὦ μοχθηρέ, παλινδορίαν παίσας αὐτοῦ καταθήσω, and adds, 'Vides versum rotundissimum, fabula ista Momothera procul ablegata'.[1]

In Athenaeus 472 D there is a fragment of Theophilus with the following reading in the MSS.:

οὐδ' ἂν Αὐτοκλῆς
Οὕτως μάτην τὴν εὐρύθμως τῇ δεξιᾷ
Ἄρασαν ὦμον.

Porson reads Οὕτως μὰ τὴν γῆν εὐρύθμως τῇ δεξιᾷ ἄρας ἐνώμα.[2]

In §§ 597 to 599 Athenaeus quotes nearly a hundred lines of a minor poet called Hermesianax. The fragment has many corruptions, and in one place appears thus in the manuscripts: οἵῳ δ' ἐχλειημένον ἔξοχον ἐχρῆν...εἶναι πολλῶν δ' ἀνθρώπων Σωκράτη ἐν σοφίῃ Κύπρις μηνίουσα πυρὸς μένει. A previous editor had suggested οἵῳ δ' ἐχλίηνεν ὄν.... Porson writes ὄν ἔξοχον ἔχρη 'Απόλλων 'Ανθρώπων εἶναι κ.τ.λ. This was one of the emendations he sent to Ruhnken as a young man; when he published

[1] Suppl. ad Praef. Hec. p. 55.

[2] Adversaria, p. 126. Schweighäuser independently conjectured μὰ τὴν γῆν and Jacobs ἄρας ἐνώμα. The former's edition of Athenaeus appeared during the latter part of Porson's life, and its new MS. evidence confirmed many of his conjectures.

it in a review he modestly gave all the credit to Wyttenbach, who had independently lighted on a similar correction.[1]

Porson had a genuine desire to discover the truth, and did not alter unless sense or metre demanded alteration. An exception seems to be in *Medea* 629, where the alteration seems especially perverse, as Porson was conscious of the objection to his proposed reading.[2] But normally he resorted to conjecture only when it was required by the rules of style and metre as he conceived them. Whether these rules were as valid as he believed is a matter of opinion. To us he may seem sometimes too ready to emend lines to make them fit his own metrical or linguistic canons.

Porson remarked of one of Dawes's rules that 'if he had been content with calling it general instead of universal it was perfectly right'.[3] The same might be said of some of Porson's own observations. He announces, for instance, the rule that after an oath such as νὴ Δία, μὰ Δία, οὐ μὰ Δία, etc., the particle γε never follows, except with another word interposed.[4] This is an interesting observation of general practice, but it is doubtful whether it should be elevated to a universal law. There are lines, not obviously corrupt, which do not conform to it. Even the famous law of the 'pause' in the fifth foot does not appear to represent a universal practice of the Greeks. The first line of the *Ion* can be made to conform by an easy transposition, but there are

[1] *Tracts and Criticisms*, p. 41; cf. p. xxxviii.
[2] Cf. *Classical Review*, xxxiv, p. 111, where Housman censures Porson for this proposal, and also for deciding that the Attic form of the 2nd sing. pres. indic. pass. ended in -ει.
[3] Letter to Dalzel, *Correspondence*, p. 89.
[4] *Adversaria*, p. 33.

lines like *Phil.* 22, *O.C.* 664, and *I.T.* 580, where the necessity of emendation is not generally admitted. And indeed Porson himself said: 'Satis ostendi ut opinor, quod promisi, paucissimos Tragicorum esse versus similes Ionis initio. Sed non ausim dicere nullos esse.'[1]

Verse composition was a pursuit in which Porson, after his undergraduate days, did not engage. We have seen how he commended Dawes for preferring the reading of good Greek to the writing of bad. Modern Greek or Latin verse was likely, he felt, to be at best a cento, and he knew too much of the language to be satisfied with what passed in his day for elegant classical verse. The pieces in *Musae Etonenses*, a collection of original Latin and Greek verses, to which he did not contribute, he described as 'trash, fit only to be put behind the fire'. These being his opinions, it is not very appropriate that he should be commemorated at Cambridge by a prize for verse composition. Yet perhaps it is not wholly inappropriate. We are told that Porson held the writing of Greek verse to be a wholesome exercise; what he objected to was the publication of such compositions. And a prize for the composition of Greek iambics commemorates the metre which he did most to illuminate. The Porson Prize marks the effects of his work, as the Browne Medals represent the interests of the pre-Porsonian period.

Before Porson the writing of Greek iambics was not much practised. Those who wrote Greek verse more often attempted hexameters and elegiacs, and even lyrics.[2] Dawes had in youth published a specimen of a translation of *Paradise Lost* into Greek hexameters,

---

[1] Suppl. ad Praef. *Hec.* p. 36.
[2] See Wordsworth, *Scholae Academicae*, p. 114.

but in later life candidly pointed out the mistakes of syntax and dialect he had committed. Porson admitted that in metre Dawes's verse was faultless; the same could not be said of another production of the period, the translation into Theocritean verse of Gray's *Elegy* by Cooke, Porson's predecessor in the Greek professorship. This set the fashion, and several other scholars published their versions of the *Elegy*. But as the century drew to a close the taste for such learned exercises passed away, and Porson's work, by setting a high standard of accuracy, made men less inclined to publish their attempts at Greek verse. At the same time his clear and convincing account of the iambic metre gave them a chance of writing verse not unlike that of the Greek tragedians, and the composition of iambics became a regular part of the English classical education.[1]

During his lifetime, Porson had never given any official teaching, had never had a pupil in the strict sense; in his last few years he had some followers among the younger Cambridge scholars, but it was after his death that he had most influence, and for several decades he dominated classical studies in the University. The best scholars of Cambridge occupied themselves with publishing his remains. He left behind him notebooks, scraps of paper and margins of books filled with his small and neat writing. These notes were collected and published with religious care by the Trinity classicists. Monk, Porson's successor in the chair of Greek, and

[1] Landor said that he and Samuel Butler were the first boys at Rugby or he believed at any other school, to attempt Greek verse (Forster, *Life of Landor*, p. 12). This same Butler, as headmaster of Shrewsbury, made Greek iambics part of his curriculum, and Kennedy even succeeded in winning the Porson Prize while still at school.

C. J. Blomfield published a volume of *Adversaria* in 1812; Dobree, who had been prevented by ill-health from assisting with the *Adversaria*, edited Porson's *Aristophanica* in 1820 and *Photius*, from his transcript, in 1822. In 1815 Kidd published in one volume a collection of his *Tracts and Miscellaneous Criticisms*.[1]

These scholars and a few others came to be recognised as a 'Porsonian school'. They were resented in some quarters as too prone to excessive admiration of Porson and of one another. According to Parr, Porson 'left his disciples scraps of Greek and cartloads of insolence'.[2] Elmsley to us may appear scarcely distinguishable from the Porsonians, but as an Oxford man he was not in the inner circle, and could write rather bitterly of the Trinity men: 'I wish you would persuade some of the *Porsonulettes* of Cambridge to review my *Oedipus Tyrannus*. . . . Having no acquaintance with *ces gens là*, I cannot ask them to do it. I wish it because I know they are in possession of the scriptures as well as the oral tradition of Porsonianism. With his mantle they possess a double portion of his spirit.'[3] The recipient of this letter, Samuel Butler of Shrewsbury, had his own reasons for disliking the Porsonians. He was an admirer of Parr, who in his old age was given to attacking Porson; he was a Johnian not a Trinity man, and he had suffered from a severe review of his *Aeschylus*[4] by C. J. Blomfield.

[1] Kidd was devoted to Greek and idolised Porson. He christened his son Richard Bentley Porson.

[2] Butler, *Life of Samuel Butler*, I, p. 66.

[3] *Id.* p. 71. Elmsley was suspected of having appropriated some of Porson's emendations. But see B. B. Rogers, *The Acharnians of Aristophanes*, p. 192 f.

[4] This was the new edition of Stanley that Porson had refused to undertake.

Blomfield had been examined by Porson for the Craven in 1806, and had won his favour by producing from memory his emendations of Aeschylus; Porson had pronounced him 'a very pretty scholar'.[1] His classical work, which ceased with his elevation to the episcopate, showed clear signs of Porson's influence; he was competent, confident and generally right; he wielded the characteristic Porsonian weapon of irony with a rather heavier hand than his master, and his unsparing reviews were apt to produce angry pamphlets from the author concerned. The best of the Porsonian school was probably Dobree, who, as we have seen, had known Porson in his last few years. Much of his short life was devoted to the study of Porson's remains, and his work, though it extended into other fields than Attic drama, followed the same methods that Porson had used. Like him, Dobree left much unpublished matter; this was collected and edited after his death by Scholefield, his successor in the professorship. But by then the Porsonian tradition was losing its vigour. Elmsley had died in the same year as Dobree, Blomfield was a busy and efficient diocesan with no time for scholarship; those who were left used Porson's method without his freshness.

Judged from the standpoint of pure classical scholarship, the middle years of the nineteenth century doubtless show a sad decline, but the classics are not made for classical scholars only, and a certain shifting of interest was natural enough, and was a reaction not so much against Porson as against an unintelligent use of his type of criticism, which had come to be regarded not only as the proper occupation of scholars but also as a good training for the youthful mind. In the University

[1] A. Blomfield, *Life of C. J. Blomfield* (ed. 1864), p. 6.

[107]

of Newton a discipline which approached the mathematical in exactness naturally found favour. 'We see', wrote Luard, himself a mathematician by profession, 'that the emending or unravelling a corrupt or hard passage of a classical author, is not mere guess or chance work, but requires as close an attention and as careful a chain of reasoning and accurate thought as a mathematical problem; and thus, that the real scholar must have been in the habit of cultivating his powers of close reasoning and accurate thought almost, if not quite, as much as the mathematician.' 'It is not difficult', he adds, 'to trace in Porson's habits of thought the influence that the study of mathematics had upon him.'[1]

It may seem to us inadequate to defend a classical education on the grounds that it is almost as good as a mathematical; and at the time that Luard wrote, even among classical scholars there were some who were abandoning this view. 'It will hardly be denied', wrote Paley in the '50's, 'that the Porsonian school of critics, much and justly as we admire their varied learning and ingenuity, have been the means of introducing into our schools a somewhat dull and dry kind of annotation useless to the mere beginner, often tiresome even to the advanced student, and fitted only for professed critics.'[2] Awed by Porson's great reputation, and taking too literally perhaps his direction 'in usum studiosae iuventutis', schoolmasters had brought up their pupils on Porson's *Euripides*, though, as Paley maintains with some justice, neither the choice of plays nor the type of annotation was suited to the young. In the '50's, it seems, it was already the fashion 'to depreciate in a

[1] *Cambridge Essays* (1857), p. 164.
[2] Paley, *Euripides*, I (1857), p. lii.

wholesale way the critical study of the classical writers, on the ground that the matter rather than the words ought to be our chief concern'.[1] Men had grown tired of a diet of *Miscellanea Critica* and the Preface to *Hecuba*. The old Porsonian scholarship yielded to a greater interest in the literary content of classical poetry, and also to the demand for a widening of the scope of classical studies. Attic poetry ceased to be so exclusively the centre of interest; men turned to the historians and the philosophers, and even to history and philosophy. Influences from Germany began to make themselves felt as our own pure scholarship lost its pre-eminence. Wolf, born in the same year as Porson, had put before the world the new science of Altertumswissenschaft, the science of antiquity, which was to study systematically all branches of knowledge connected with the ancient world. Archaeology, philosophy, mythology, philology began to demand the attention of the scholar, and to claim equal importance with the old study of texts, which itself began to appear unscientific in view of increased knowledge of MSS.

But to discuss these later developments is no part of this work. It is not our business to write a history of classical scholarship since Porson, to measure it by his standard, to approve or disapprove either of him or of our recent scholars. It is enough to suggest that Porson's influence on our education and scholarship has been considerable, and that it may still be felt, though faintly, at the present day. It would be a mistake to over-emphasise the importance of a single man, but it is at least in part due to Porson that Greek occupies the place it does in our education, and that Attic literature holds

[1] Paley, *Aeschylus* (1855), p. ix.

[109]

a firm and central position in our classical scholarship. (It would be interesting to know when Plutarch ceased to be read.) With more certainty we may set down as due to Porson the fact that so many young men learn to write Greek iambics, and write them tolerably well.

But Porson is not to be judged primarily by the extent of his influence. 'Non quantum quisque prosit sed quanti quisque sit ponderandum.' He should be remembered as a great scholar who knew Greek as few if any others have known it, and also as a man gifted with wit and character, something more than a mere academic figure, and more than a mere eccentric.

APPENDIX

A. LETTERS OF PORSON
PREVIOUSLY UNPUBLISHED

I. TO DAVID RUHNKEN[1]

Viro longe doctissimo Davidi Ruhnkenio
Ricardus Porson S.

Quas ad me rescripsisti humanitatis plenissimas literas, incredibile dictu est, Vir amplissime, quanta me voluptate affecerint; non quo dignum me ipse putem laudibus iis, quibus me benigne ornasti, sed quod meam de literis humanioribus bene merendi voluntatem boni consulueris, et quos in primis studiorum meorum rudimentis parvos quosdam ingenii igniculos vidisse visus es, fovere et ventilare dignatus sis. Quod autem me nunc potissimum impulit ut tibi scriberem, hoc est. Pollicitus es literis tuis te ex Grammaticis ineditis quorum copiam habes Aeschyli fragmenta in gratiam meam descripturum. Id ut nunc praestes rogo. Idem juvenis qui hanc epistolam in manus tuas tradet, quicquid ejus fidei committas, ad me perferendum pro humanitate sua suscepit. Sed hoc onus tibi, Vir egregie, impono ea exceptione, si neq; per valetudinem neque per negotium impediris. Illud etiam, si potes, adjuvato ut si qua Aeschyli loca quae in integris fabulis extant aliter quam in editis leguntur, eorum varias lectiones adscribas. Probe enim tu, si quis alius, nosti, quantum saepe in levissima varietate momentum situm sit. Viden qualem a te operam exigere ausus sim? Sed quoniam iam bene et gnaviter oportet esse impudentem, tua ipsius humanitas, qui nugas meas tam comiter exceperis, in causa est, cur tanto opere tibi molestus sim. Vale, Vir summe, et rem feliciter gere. Dabam Coll. Trin: Cantab. Jul. 4. 1785.

[1] From Trin. Coll. collection. See p. 15.

[111]

P.S. Cum chartae aliquid superest, tempora tua paulisper diutius occupare decrevi. De ἐκτήσαντο in Hermesianacte quamvis forsan quaedam pro sententia mea dicere possem, de talibus tamen vix cum quoquam alio, nedum tecum contenderim. Sed quod ad posteriorem locum attinet, nondum induci possum, ut in emendatione mea vel apicem mutandum censeam.[1] Ordo enim verborum, quem Wyttenbachius sequitur, in nullo codice comparet; quem ego sequor, longe numerosiorem versum facit, et a MS. Veneto confirmatur; deinde proclive erat librariis ἔχρη in ἐχρῆν mutare, cum prius eo sensu et forma adeo rarum sit, ut tribus tantum in locis invenerim. Sophocl. Elect. init. ΧΡΗ μοι τοιαῦθ᾿ ὁ Φοῖβος. Oed. Col. τὰ πόλλ᾿ ἐκεῖν᾿ ὅτ᾿ ΕΞΕΧΡΗ κακά. Apollon. Rhod. 1. 302. ἐπεὶ μάλα δεξιὰ Φοῖβος ΕΧΡΗ. Illud etiam non omittendum duxi, si quid forte tua interest, prodiisse non diu post Epistolarum tuarum repetitam editionem pusilli, si quid ego judico, critici libellum, (Steph. Weston nomine) quo hoc Hermesianactis fragmentum emaculare conatur.[2] Sed unam tantummodo ibi conjecturam, quam probarem, repperi. Ea est vs. 84, ubi legit, Οὐδ᾿ ΟΙΔ᾿ ΑΙΝΟΝ Ἔρωτος—quod a MS. Veneto aliquatenus confirmatur. Sed prolixae epistolae jam finem faciam, postquam conjecturas aliquot in Aeschyli Supplices tecum communicarim. Rationes omisi tum ut brevitati consulerem, tum quod eae, quibus vis aut pondus insit, sponte tibi occurrent.

Suppl. 69. Ὤλετο πρὸς χειρὸς ΕΘΕΝ.

325–6. Δαναὸς· ἀδελφὸς δ᾿ ἐστὶ
   πεντηκοντάπαις—   καὶ τοῦ δαναοίγε
  ΒΑΣ. Καὶ ΤΟΥΔ᾿ ΑΝΟΙΓΕ   Ald. Robort.
  τοὔνομ᾿ εὐφώνῳ λόγῳ.

686. *seq.* Μηδέ τις ἀνδροκμὴς | Λοιγὸς ἐπελθέτω | Τάνδε πόλιν ΔΑΙΖΩΝ | ΑΧΟΡΟΝ ΑΚΙΘΑΡΙΝ | Δακρυογόνον Ἄρην | Βοάν τ᾿ ΕΝΔΗΜΟΝ ΕΞΟΠΛΙΖΩΝ. Confer et emenda Plutarchum in Erotico.

See p. 102.   [2] See p. 18.

II. TO MRS HEWITT[1]

Dear Madam,

I was equally surprized and obliged the other day with the favour of a letter from you; surprized at the unexpected subject; obliged by your candour in charitably supposing (what was indeed the truth) that I had not received your former. Perhaps you made some mistake in the direction. The people here are so ignorant or negligent that they cannot or will not always find out apartments that are not very punctually described in the direction. So that I rather the less wonder your letter should miss me, since some others have lately had the same fate. But I am still more obliged to you for the zeal you show in behalf of my brother, though with respect to the particular object of his expedition, I am in great doubt whether it will prove of any use. At least I do not see of what use I can be to him, whether I consider myself as examiner or patron. As an examiner, I am scarcely qualified to judge of the precise quantity of knowledge necessary to fit my brother for the situation he wishes to obtain. For I am entirely destitute of that professional experience which I should think an indispensable requisite towards passing a fair judgment. If your Mr Hewitt gave his testimony in Thomas's favour, I should for this reason be much readier to pin my faith upon his evidence than trust to my own opinion. But if my brother wants my influence and recommendation to assist him, he could not unfortunately have pitched upon a person either with less intelligence or with less interest. The only schools I know are three. Of these Eton and Westminster are entirely out of the question; in the third there is at present no vacancy, and if there were, I fear Thomas's age would be an insuperable objection. At present I know of no other place, nor am I likely to be in the way of knowing. However I shall certainly direct my attention for the future to enquiries of this sort, and the little

---

[1] From Trin. Coll. collection. See p. 61.

ability I have shall be exert in his favour. In the meantime I have taken the liberty to mention him to Dr Parr,
who may probably have it sooner in his power to serve
us, than we to serve ourselves. Excepting him, I have
not a single acquaintance upon whose information or
assistance I could reasonably build the least hope. Dr
Parr has been so good as to promise to take our case
into consideration, and if the prospect clears, the light
will shine from this quarter. I have examined my
brother a little; the reason I have already hinted makes
me believe any thing more unnecessary for the present
at least. Besides the different plans of conducting
different schools, the different departments of different
assistances, and other circumstances, would prevent me
from making any positive and final decision. However
I should not hesitate, I think, to recommend him as an
assistant to teach the rudiments of Latin and perhaps
of Greek, in a grammar school. If he were lucky enough
soon to obtain such an establishment, and employ due
care to improve his present stock, in two or three years
he might probably soar somewhat higher, and what now
strikes me as the grandest objection, his age, would be
less exceptionable. The best time I should think for a
more strict examination will be when we actually know
of a vacancy, and can therefore tell to a certainty what
demands will be made as well as how we are likely to
satisfy them. I had much more to say on this subject,
but I have already tired you, I am afraid, with what
I have written. Give me leave therefore to thank you
again for the very obliging concern you have manifested
in my brother's welfare, and I shall conclude with
desiring my best compliments to Mr Hewitt, and assuring
you that I am,

Dear Madam,

Your very obliged

humble servant,

R. PORSON.

Essex Court, Middle Temple, No. 5.
Apr. 24, 1788.

III. TO CHARLES BURNEY[1]

Dear Burney,

I have been silent, because I have had nothing to say, which, I think, your philosophers hold to be a prudent measure. Send me a copy of that same conspectus, if you can, by return of post. As to Burgess's publishing Photius, he may do it, if he pleases, but then I should imagine, the best way is what I am going to propose. Let him get out of some library at Oxford the imperfect copy of Photius, which they have, and send it to me; I have now the MS by me, and will send him an exact collation. I could do it, I make no doubt, in a week. I sent 'Squire Ralphs a line a day or two agone, in which I informed him that he should have the *conclusion*, if *that* could be, before the end of the week.[2] I shall refer to Maffei in it, so you will transcribe what may be necessary, and put it in the form of a note. Did you see the author's card? I thought he seemed somewhat afraid. I shall be suaviter in modo, but I fear there is no avoiding fortiter in re. I must sweeten him with a few compliments, and humbly conceive with all possible submission, that he is entirely in the wrong. Moreover I should like to see that same Pinelli catalogue. Send a copy of it with the conspectus, if it be published. They will very conveniently accompany each other in the same parcel. I cannot at present tell for certain whether I shall send off my review of the dissertation to-morrow or on Friday. But if you can peep into it before you go to Oxford, so much the better; and if anything occurs to you, either of correction, addition or subtraction, let

---

[1] From the original in the possession of Mr J. H. A. Sparrow.

[2] Porson refers here and in the next letter to his review of Robertson's *Dissertation on the Parian Chronicle, The Monthly Review*, October 1788 and January 1789 (Kidd, *Tracts and Criticisms*, p. 57).

it be amended, inserted, or expunged accordingly. So
no more at present from

Yours etc.

R. PORSON.

T.C. 17 Dec. 1788.

IV. TO CHARLES BURNEY[1]

Dear Burney,

I could certainly have given my author another *knock
or two*, but I thought it would be a transgression of that
neutrality which ought to be preserved in a review.
Yet I thought I had given him some smart touches, but
perhaps my ridicule was too feeble and remote. Else
I suppose you might have perceived something of this
kind in the sentence of my first part beginning, 'We
cannot help observing'[2]—and in that sentence of my
second that contains an elaborate arithmetical calculation.[3] If any separate argument has been entirely
omitted, I do hereby empower you to add it. With
respect to ἀνέβη the aorist is rarely if ever used in prose,
and has an active sense. The same distinction is observed
between ἔστην and ἔστησα. I shall review Hewlett's
book, if Griffiths pleases.[4] The Photius you mention is
written either in the latter end of the last or in the present
century. The Aristophanes is a very good MS, it is,
if I remember, No. 27, and I have collated it with great
accuracy. I shall write to Ruhnkenius as soon as possible.
By the way if the said Photius is not soon sent, it need
not be sent at all, because I shall shortly be in town.
As for the Pinelli catalogue, I shall say nothing to it.

[1] From the original in the possession of Mr J. H. A. Sparrow.
[2] *The Monthly Review*, October 1788, p. 352.
[3] Kidd, *Tracts and Criticisms*, p. 76.
[4] Ralph Griffiths, proprietor of *The Monthly Review*. Hewlett's
Vindication of the Authenticity of the Parian Chronicle was reviewed
by Porson, December 1791.

People of my limited income, must not expect that their pittance of 900 or 1000 pounds per annum will purchase every expensive book. You have said nothing about Schroder's Observations, whether Elmsly has any more copies etc. I mention this because Whiter would like a copy, if it can be procured. I suppose you will communicate this to Mr Griffiths, whose letters I have received. Read the Gentleman's Magazine for October and December. So no more at present, but rests

Yours

R. PORSON.

13 Jan., 1789.

V. TO CHARLES BURNEY[1]

Dear Burney,

Tell those learned men the Printers or Booksellers or by whatever name they more willingly hear, that I am not unwilling to undertake this business.[2] But tell them at the same time that I cannot be in town in less than ten days from this present date. If these worthy Messrs will allow this delay, I am, to a certain degree, at their service. Mr Banks desires his compliments and I believe will send you a brother of his, if he can, *but this is a secret*. You will let me know by return of post or at least as soon as you can, what is done or may be done about this business. Mr Langton is here, (i.e. in this room)[3] and in good spirits, but that learned lady, Miss Langton, is at Bath. I am not clear whether I answered all the questions in your letter, but these we shall settle at another meeting. Yours therefore sincerely

R. PORSON.

9 March, 1791.

---

[1] From the original in the possession of Mr J. H. A. Sparrow.
[2] Probably the edition of Aeschylus, see p. 65.
[3] Written over 'here'.

VI. TO MRS HAWES[1]

Essex Court, No. 5, Middle Temple,
March 18, 1794.

Dear Sister,

I want a certificate of my baptism from the parish register as soon as possibly it can be got. I have taken the liberty to apply to you, rather than send to Ruston round by N. Walsham, not knowing how long it might be in travelling that way. An exact copy of the entry in the register, signed by the minister, will, I believe, be sufficient. I think no stamp is necessary. When you get it, I shall be much obliged to you, if you send it off to Norwich by the first opportunity. You may perhaps wish to know why I am in such a hurry. I really cannot exactly tell myself, but as soon as I do, you shall immediately be informed. I rely on your zeal and affection for executing the commission with which I have troubled you, and remain,

[Signature cut out]

P.S. My respects and duty to your whole family.

VII. TO JAMES PERRY[2]

Dear Perry,

I called upon Dr Cory,[3] who gave me to understand, that he was not bursar, and that the bursar was then absent from college, but that he should see him in the course of a week. He rather thought however that Mr Cole had in 1799 renewed his lease for 21 years. In the memorandum-book Mr Cole renews his lease of the farm at Mitcham, which he took to comprehend all

---

[1] From Trin. Coll. collection.
[2] From Trin. Coll. collection.
[3] Master of Emmanuel. Cf. *Correspondence*, p. 70.

the premises that Mr Cole held of the college. But late last night I received a note from Dr Cory, stating that he was mistaken; for that Mr Cole was now in treaty with the bursar for the meadow lands, and desiring me to advise you to apply with all speed to their sollicitor Mr Nichols, No. 88, Queen Street, Cheapside. As hours may in this case be of consequence, I send this by the Telegraph. In the mean time I wish you would at your leisure look out that number of the Chronicle that has the version of 'Three Children', and send it down hither.[1] If you break the file, I will carefully keep the number and restore it. I am just sending back the first sheets of the Medea, and I fancy I shall henceforth be fully employed. I remain therefore with respects and love to the rest of the people,

Dear Perry,

Yours sincerely,

R. PORSON.

Trin: Coll:
30 May, 1801.

VIII. TO MRS HAWES[2]

Dear Sister,

I received yours this morning, to which you desire an immediate answer, and that will be scarce time enough, unless by Wednesday you mean Wednesday se'nnight. I meant to have been in Norfolk long before now, but one avocation or another, especially of late, has hindered me. I expect in the course of a few days to be at Cambridge, and after a week or a fortnight's stay there to take a trip to Coltishall; in the meantime, if Mr Hawes will be so good as advance me twenty pounds to be disposed of towards our niece's benefit, as he and you and Mr Brown shall agree, tell him I will faithfully

---

[1] See p. 72.   [2] From Trin. Coll. collection.

restore him that sum and his great coat the next time
I have the pleasure of seeing him. I am with proper
remembrances to all friends,

Dear Sister,

Your affectionate brother,

R. PORSON.

29 July, 1806.

If you write to me in town,
direct, at the London Institution, No. 8 Old Jewry. I
shall probably leave London
next Monday.

P.S. Tell Squire Siday I
    have not forgotten him.

IX. TO MRS HAWES[1]

Dear Sister,

I purpose, if no impediment take place, to set out from
Cambridge tomorrow, whence I expect to reach Newmarket about four in the afternoon. There I shall go
early to bed in order to go with the coach, which I
understand passes through Newmarket about three in
the morning, and will get into Norwich, I suppose,
between eleven and twelve. It stops at the White Hart,
Newmarket; so you can easily, I imagine, find out where
it inns at Norwich, if you can make it convenient to
meet me. With due remembrances to your family and
our other friends I remain,

Dear Sister,

Your loving brother,

R. PORSON.

Trin: Coll.
25 Aug. 1806.

[1] From Trin. Coll. collection.

[120]

X. TO MATTHEW RAINE[1]

Dear Doctor,

I hope you have left all people in the north quite well, and are returned you and Miss Raine with a fresh stock of health and spirits to support the fatigues of the ensuing campaign. Mr Nares of the Museum informs me that he has had some discourse with his brother officers, and they think with him, that if the trustees of the Museum were induced to consider the Dorvillian MSS a proper κειμήλιον for that repository, an application to Parliament would obtain the grant of a sum sufficient for the purchase. I should think too that such an agreement, if it could take place, would not be displeasing to you or Banks. At any rate you can call upon Mr Nares, and let him know whether you are willing to treat, or open to any treaty, or already too much engaged in another. If it is necessary to write to Banks on the occasion, will you send him a line on the subject by the first opportunity. Mr Perry will bring this to town which you would have received sooner, but I have been too ill to take a pen in hand. I am, with all needful compliments,

Dear Doctor,

Yours sincerely,

R. PORSON.

Little Hermitage near
Rochester, Kent. 14 June [? 1807[2]]

The bride and bridegroom desire their best compliments.

[1] From a copy in Luard's *Correspondence of Porson* in Trin. Coll. Library.
[2] Cf. *Correspondence*, p. 112.

B. BIBLIOGRAPHIES

BIOGRAPHICAL

The following are the main sources for Porson's Life:

The Gentleman's Magazine, September, October, 1808.

The Athenaeum, October, November, December, 1808.

The Monthly Magazine, November, 1808.

JAMES SAVAGE, Account of the last illness of Richard Porson, in *The Librarian*, 1808.

ADAM CLARKE, *Narrative of the last illness and Death of Richard Porson*, 1808.

The above are reprinted in Barker's *Literary Anecdotes*, vol. II; see below.

STEPHEN WESTON (?), *A Short Account of the late Mr Porson*, 1808. Reprinted in 1814 with Τεμάχη, or *Scraps from Porson's Rich Feast*.

THOMAS KIDD, *Imperfect Outline of the Life of Richard Porson*, and Preface, prefixed to Porson's *Tracts and Criticisms*, 1815.

WILLIAM BELOE, *The Sexagenarian*, 1817.

The New Monthly Magazine, June, 1820.

E. H. BARKER, *Parriana*, vol. II, 1828.

PRYSE LOCKHART GORDON, *Personal Memoirs*, 1830.

E. H. BARKER, *Literary Anecdotes*, 1852.

—— *Porsoniana* in MS. in Trinity College Library, Cambridge.

MALTBY, *Porsoniana* in Samuel Rogers's *Table Talk* (ed. Dyce), 1856.

Art. Porson in Knight's *English Encyclopaedia* 1857 (by Porson's nephew Hawes).

H. R. LUARD, Richard Porson, in *Cambridge Essays*, 1857.

SAMUEL ROGERS, *Recollections*, 1859.

JOHN SELBY WATSON, *Life of Porson*, 1861.

Correspondence of Porson, ed. Luard, 1867 (Cambridge Anti-
quarian Society Publications, VIII).
H. J. NICOLL, *Great Scholars*, 1880.
R. C. JEBB in *Dictionary of National Biography*.
J. E. SANDYS, *History of Classical Scholarship*, vol. II, 1906.
E. J. MARTIN in *The Church Quarterly Review*, October 1932.

For other sources besides these I have given references in
footnotes.

PORSON'S WRITINGS

This list is not exhaustive. It does not include trivial
productions, and those of uncertain authorship.

Maty's New Review, June 1783. Review of the second part
of vol. I of Schütz's *Aeschylus*. (*Classical Journal*, Sep-
tember 1813; Porson's *Tracts and Criticisms*, p. 4.)
The Same, July 1783. Review of Brunck's *Aristophanes*.
(*Classical Journal*, March 1813; *Tracts and Criticisms*,
p. 11; *Museum Criticum*, V, 1826.)
The Same, April 1784. Review of Weston's *Hermesianax*.
(*Tracts and Criticisms*, p. 38.)
The Same, August 1784. Review of Huntingford's *Apology
for the Monostrophics*. (*Tracts and Criticisms*, p. 48.)
The Same, April 1785. The learned pig. (*Tracts and Criticisms*,
p. 54.)
The Same, April 1786. Original unedited letters between
Le Clerc and Bentley.
Notes appended to the Cambridge edition of Hutchinson's
Anabasis of Xenophon, 1786.
The Gentleman's Magazine, August, September and October,
1787. Three letters signed Sundry Whereof, on
Hawkins's *Life of Johnson*. (*Tracts and Criticisms*, p. 333;
Correspondence of Porson, p. 7.)
The Same, October 1788. Letter signed Cantabrigiensis on
Beza's MS. and Dr Kipling. (*Correspondence*, p. 23.)

The Same, December 1788, February, April, May, June and August, 1789. Six letters signed Cantabrigiensis, on the authenticity of 1 John v. 7, and Mr Travis's defence of the verse. (Reprinted with additions in the *Letters to Travis*.)

The Monthly Review, October 1788 and January 1789. Review of Robertson's *Dissertation on the Parian Chronicle*. (The second article reprinted in *Museum Criticum*, II, 1814, and *Tracts and Criticisms*, p. 57.)

The Gentleman's Magazine, February 1790. Reproof Valiant to Mr Travis's Reply Churlish. (*Tracts and Criticisms*, p. 352; *Correspondence*, p. 34.)

Letters to Mr Archdeacon Travis in answer to his defence of the three heavenly witnesses, 1 John v. 7, 1790. (*Classical Journal*, December 1827, March, June, September and December, 1828, March 1829.)

Notes appended to Toup's *Emendationes in Suidam*, Oxford 1790. (Written 1787.)

The Monthly Review, December 1791. Review of Hewlett's *Vindication of the Authenticity of the Parian Chronicle*.

A new Catechism for the use of the Swinish Multitude, 1792.

Virgilii Opera, ed. Heyne, London 1793, corrected for the press by Porson with preface Corrector lectori. (*Tracts and Criticisms*, p. 103.)

The Monthly Review, July 1793. Review of Edwards's *Plutarch De Educatione Puerorum*. (*Tracts and Criticisms*, p. 84.)

The Morning Chronicle, Nov. 21 and Dec. 27, 1793, Sept. 27, 1794. Three letters signed Mythologus on the *Orgies of Bacchus*. (*Spirit of the Public Journals*, 1797, p. 261.)

The Monthly Review, January and April, 1794. Review of Payne Knight's *Analytical Essay on the Greek Alphabet*. (*Museum Criticum*, IV, 1814; *Tracts and Criticisms*, p. 108.)

The Morning Chronicle, June 25, Aug. 12, and Sept. 13, 1794. Three imitations of Horace. (*Spirit of the Public Journals*, 1797, pp. 107, 147; *Classical Journal*, Sept. 1811.)

[125]

Αἱ τοῦ Αἰσχύλου Τραγῳδίαι ἑπτά. Glasgow, 1795.
The Morning Chronicle, April 13, 1796. Letter signed S.
England. (*Tracts and Criticisms*, p. 154; *Correspondence*,
p. 60.)
Euripidis Hecuba, 1797.
Euripidis Orestes, 1798. (Reprinted 1811, 1818, 1848.)
Euripidis Phoenissae, 1799. (Reprinted 1811, 1818, 1848.)
Collation of the Harleian MS. of the *Odyssey* appended to the
Grenville *Homer*, Oxford 1801.
Euripidis Medea, Cambridge, 1801. (Reprinted, London,
1812, 1817, 1829, 1847.)
Euripidis Hecuba, Cambridge, 1802. Second edition with
Supplement to the Preface. (Reprinted, London, 1808,
1825, 1847.)
Euripidis Tragoediae, I (Porson's four plays), Leipzig, 1802.
(Reprinted 1807, 1824.)
The Monthly Magazine, December 1802. Letter signed John
Nic. Dawes. (*Tracts and Criticisms*, p. 151; *Correspondence*
p. 78.)
Aeschyli Tragoediae, London, 1806 (printed Glasgow, 1794).

POSTHUMOUS PUBLICATIONS

Adversaria, ed. Monk and Blomfield, Cambridge, 1812.
(Reprinted, Leipzig, 1814.)
Archaeologia, 1812, contains Porson's Restoration of the Greek
inscription on the Rosetta Stone, from a communication
to the Society of Antiquaries made in 1803. (*Tracts and
Criticisms*, p. 183.)
Museum Criticum, III, 1814. Letter to Andrew Dalzel, 1803,
published by James Tate. (*Correspondence*, p. 85.)
Tracts and Miscellaneous Criticisms of Richard Porson, ed.
Kidd, 1815. (The Preface contains a bibliography of
Porson's works, including publications of others to which
he contributed notes.)

Aristophanica (including text of the Plutus), ed. Dobree, Cambridge, 1820.

Notes on Pausanias appended to Gaisford's *Lectiones Platonicae*, Oxford, 1820.

Φωτίου τοῦ πατριάρχου λέξεων συναγωγή *e codice* Galeano *descripsit Ricardus Porsonus*, ed. Dobree, Cambridge, 1822.

Euripidis Tragoediae priores quattuor, ed. Scholefield, Cambridge, 1826. (Reprinted 1829, 1851.)

The four plays were edited by J. R. Major for school use with the notes translated into English, the *Hecuba* in 1826, the other three in 1830.

Praelection on Euripides, reprinted from *Adversaria*, Cambridge, 1828.

Notes on Suidas appended to Gaisford's edition, 1834.

Correspondence of Porson, ed. H. R. Luard, Cambridge, 1867.

INDEX

For EU product safety concerns, contact us at Calle de José Abascal, 56–1°,
28003 Madrid, Spain or eugpsr@cambridge.org.

www.ingramcontent.com/pod-product-compliance
Ingram Content Group UK Ltd.
Pitfield, Milton Keynes, MK11 3LW, UK
UKHW020314140625
459647UK00018B/1864